# Gene Nelson

Lights! Camera! Dance!

By Scott O'Brien

Typesetting and layout by PKJ Passion Global

Published in the USA by
BearManor Media
1317 Edgewater Dr #110
Orlando FL 32804
www.BearManorMedia.com

Softcover Edition
ISBN-10:
ISBN-13: 979-8-88771-252-9

Published in the USA by Bear Manor Media

## Also by Scott O'Brien

*Kay Francis—I Can't Wait to be Forgotten* (2006)
> *Classic Images Magazine*—"Best Books of 2006" Laura Wagner—
> "O'Brien has a way with words as he beautifully examines Kay's films. He skillfully uses Kay's own diary to paint a picture of an independent woman ahead of her time."

*Virginia Bruce—Under My Skin* (2008)
> *Daeida Magazine*—David Ybarra (editor)—"*Under My Skin* is a well-researched, tactful, and skilled examination into the tragedy of a talented, beautiful and popular figure in film history, desperate to fall in love at any cost. Highly recommended."

*Ann Harding—Cinema's Gallant Lady* (2010)
> *San Francisco Gate*—Mick LaSalle—"Scott O'Brien has managed to come up with a thick, fact-filled, smart and very readable biography of this enormous talent. Harding deserves to be known, and the public deserves to know her."

*Ruth Chatterton—Actress, Aviator, Author* (2013)
> *Huffington Post*—Thomas Gladys—"Best Film Books of 2013"

*George Brent—Ireland's Gift to Hollywood and its Leading Ladies* (2014)
> *Classic Images* —Laura Wagner—"One of my favorites, Scott O'Brien, has written another excellent biography. O'Brien etches a fascinating portrait. His sources are

extensive and, unlike hack writers, O'Brien provides pages of documentation."

*Sylvia Sidney—Paid by the Tear* (2016)
*Sight & Sound*—Dan Callahan—"O'Brien has labored to find the surviving people who worked with Sidney. Comments from these co-workers add texture to her story. O'Brien's book provides welcome insight into the jabbing toughness Sidney needed ... to survive in show business as long as she did."

*Herbert Marshall - A Biography* (2018)
Stephen Michael Shearer (author of *Gloria Swanson - The Ultimate Star*)
"I will read *anything* by author Scott O'Brien. O'Brien's approach to his subject matter is concise and sensitive. With *Herbert Marshall - A Biography*, the author has given us another landmark publication of one of Hollywood's best loved actors."

*Elissa Landi – Cinema's Empress of Emotion* (2020)
*Classic Images* – "Best Books of 2021" Laura Wagner – In my opinion, O'Brien's best yet. Landi had a much more interesting life than many other Hollywood actresses. Scott, a marvelous writer, brings Landi alive in these pages.

# Table of Contents

**1947 publicity shot -** *I Wonder Who's Kissing Her Now?* **(Fox)**

# Foreword: Gene Nelson – Master of Dance and Transition

In 1949, Gene Nelson and his dazzling, athletic, unique dance style, arrived at Warner Brothers. Prior to this, Gene honed his skills in venues that would surprise many. What got the proverbial ball rolling, however, does not come as a surprise. In the 1980's, Nelson recalled going to the Wilshire Theatre in Santa Monica to see *Flying Down to Rio* with Fred Astaire. "It stoned me," Gene admitted. "I came out of that theater flying, and dancing all the way home. I was so impressed with Astaire … I told my family I had to be a dancer."[1]

While Astaire inspired, it was Sonja Henie & Co. who took Gene under their wing. At eighteen, he fell in love with ice-skating, spending all his spare time at Hollywood's Polar Palace. Three months later, he auditioned for the Sonja Henie Ice Revue. He was hired! His lean good looks and muscular frame (yes, he liked to hang out at Santa Monica's famous Muscle Beach), were also in his favor. He was in the chorus of two Henie films: *Second Fiddle* (1939), and *Everything Happens at Night* (1939). Gene realized that ballet training would further enhance his skating skill, and took private lessons from Bert Prival who had danced with the Metropolitan Opera. "And boy did he work me over," Nelson laughed, "Whew! We became very, very close friends."[2]

With the demanding technique of ballet in queue, Gene was a standout in the Sonja Henie revue *It Happens on Ice*. His astonishing moves proved that he feared *nothing*. While he was playing in Manhattan, one lovely fan, a talented dancer in her own right, came back stage to meet him. The attraction was mutual. Between sledding in Central Park and snowball fights, Gene and Miriam teamed up to dance on celluloid for the popular 1941 "Soundie" (a jukebox with a screen) *Boardwalk Boogie*. It came as no surprise when they tied the marital knot two weeks after Pearl Harbor was bombed. Gene was twenty-one.

At the outbreak of WWII, it was composer Irving Berlin who latched onto Gene. "I enlisted in the Signal Corps," said Nelson, who liked to tap dance around the base with his portable radio. "I was really lucky. I appeared in one of the [Army] Post talent shows. Ezra Stone [director] and Irving Berlin were canvassing all the various camps. The following morning, I got orders to transfer to Long Island for tour duty in *This is the Army*."[3] The show had a popular SRO six months stay on Broadway, before touring the U.S. Occasionally, Gene took the opportunity, albeit less enthusiastically, to explore his feminine side. A few of the numbers in *This is the Army* had troops perform in drag. Private Leander Berg (Gene's birthname) revealed to a D.C. reporter, "People are so surprised to see how well we do as girls, that they think we are better than we are." Pvt. Berg admitted that he felt sorry for female thespians. "It's so much trouble," he complained. "All that stuff on their faces, and those frail little dresses."[4]

**1942 - *This is the Army* "A Soldier's Dream" - Joe Johnson, Robert Sidney, Phillip Wernick, Pvt. Gene Berg, Nelson Barclift (on the floor) was the lover of Cole Porter at the time.**

During 1943, the troops filmed a Hollywood production of *This is the Army* at Warner Bros. Private First-Class Gene Berg showed up in several sequences. After Hollywood, *This is the Army* spent two years overseas. Gene coupled his dancing skill with military duty, as a steamship operator and 20mm gunner. *This is the Army* was the only integrated unit in the Armed Forces (per Berlin's insistence). Gene Nelson took integration a step further. Although the African-American and white troops traveled and lived together, the musical numbers were not integrated. When a small *This is the Army* division headed to Algiers, stage manager Alan Anderson appointed Gene as team captain. Nelson took the opportunity to select eight other dancers to perform alongside him. Three of them were African-American.[5] Most likely, it was the only *truly* inter-racial episode for *This is the Army*. The troops took their final bow in Honolulu, October 22, 1945.

Over the years, Gene Nelson welcomed the opportunity for new ventures. Undeterred by a broken back, and Hollywood's oversight in not offering him more leading roles, Gene graciously explored what life offered. He directed film noir, sci-fi, and two films starring Elvis Presley. He was behind the camera for dozens of popular TV shows – including an episode of the original *Star Trek*. Nelson taught Theatre Arts at my alma mater, San Francisco State University. Yep. Gene Nelson's later career was filled with as many surprises as his early beginnings - a true master of dance *and* transition.

# Chapter 1

# Roots: "The Apple Didn't Fall Far from the Tree"

*Gene Nelson (1982)*

Gene Nelson came by his ability for transition naturally. His father, Leander Esaias Berg, born in 1885, left behind his Swedish roots at the age of 16. With $30 in his pocket, he traveled from the hamlet of Lännäs, near Sweden's Lake Hjälmaren, to the United States, arriving in May 1901. In 1916, Leander became a naturalized U.S. citizen. A natural athlete, he performed as an acrobat with a troop centered in Chicago, but his main trade was as a machinist. Leander returned to Sweden in the autumn of 1916, to look after his ailing, widowed mother, Anna Sofia. Two years later, Leander's September 1918 draft registration would confirm that he brought Anna back to the United States, where she resided in Astoria, Oregon. His brother Carl, also a machinist, lived nearby. By that time, Leander, who did not enter the military, was employed as a machinist and working in Alaska.

**Leander Berg – passport photo (1916)**

On December 29, 1918, at the age of 33, Leander married a 20-year-old woman who was born in Astoria in 1898. She also had Swedish roots. Her name was Lenore Christine Nelson. Lenore's father John, and mother Ingaborg Bakke Nelson, had immigrated from Sweden and Norway, respectively. John, a fisherman for many years, was a local celebrity of sorts. As a champion submarine diver, he made news on several occasions. His skill in underwater detection of damaged ship hulls, gained him much respect and admiration. On December 9, 1901 his celebrity came to a bitter end. Lenore was three-years-old at the time.

*The Morning Astorian* headlined: "Diver J.O. Nelson Made a Successful Effort at Suicide Last Evening". The report detailed,

> *After making an almost successful attempt upon the life of his wife, J.O. Nelson, the well-known diver, last night stabbed himself through the heart and died within a few minutes. Jealousy prompted the terrible deed.*[6]

# DROVE A KNIFE INTO HIS HEART

---

### Diver J. O. Nelson Made a Successful Effort at Suicide Last Evening.

---

## HE TRIED TO KILL HIS WIFE

---

In a Fit of Jealousy, the Man Attacked and Wounded Her and Then Ended His Own Existence.

***The Morning Astorian*** **(December 10, 1901)**

Neighbors indicated that the couple frequently quarreled. As Ingaborg was a devoted wife and mother, it was difficult to understand her husband's sullen moods and temperament. After being stabbed with a six-inch gash down the back of her neck, Ingaborg was fortunate to escape John's wrath and run to a neighbor's house. While her two brothers were asleep upstairs, little Lenore fled home through the back door. Police were summoned. Upon arrival, they found her father's body. A close friend of John, told reporters that he had "been acting queerly of late." Another report indicated that he was intoxicated.[7] Even so, such blood-curdling tragedy was unexpected. A memorial service was held three days later. A local organization called The Workmen, compensated Ingaborg and her children with $2,000. She never remarried.

After completing high school, Lenore found employment at Astoria's Beehive Dept. Store. Her marriage to Leander helped her leave the past behind. By 1920, they relocated 180 miles north to reside in Seattle, Washington, where their son Eugene Leander Berg was born on March 24, 1920.[8] Baby Eugene's only living grandparent was Ingaborg Nelson. Anna Sophia Berg had passed away on Christmas Day 1919. In 1921, Leander and Lenore returned to Astoria for one year, where grandmother Nelson got to bond with her young grandson.

In 1990, Gene detailed that by 1924, he and his parents resided on Orange Grove Avenue in Los Angeles. "During the early part of our stay," he said, "jobs weren't too easy to find. So, dad answered a call at the Douglas Fairbanks studios [Pickford-Fairbanks Studios] to be an extra. Five dollars a day and a box lunch. It was better than nothing. He was trying to feed his family, right?"[9] Leander worked for one week. Dressed in rags, he was lost among a thousand extras for Fairbanks' *The Thief of Bagdad.* "It was very exciting," Gene nodded, "because when the picture did come out, we all had to run to go see dad. The shot came that he was in. A sea of people. You couldn't tell one from the other. But it was fun just knowing he was there." On screen, Fairbanks' "agility and natural grace" (as Gene put it) would prove to be an inspiration for Leander's son.

Before long, Leander, along with his brother Carl, signed on as machinists for Douglas Aircraft, headquartered in Santa Monica. After completing a global journey around the world in 1924, the company had become a major world aerospace manufacturer.

1930. The Bergs lived in an apartment on Santa Monica's 17th Street. The census indicated they had a radio! As the Depression surged, Leander was fortunate to have a steady, reliable income. Son Eugene attended McKinley School, where he took an interest in the school newspaper. He was on the McKinley newspaper committee.[10] It was a pursuit that he would carry over into high school. The coastal city of Santa Monica was surrounded by the film capital: Hollywood, Beverly Hills … a film afficionado's paradise.

As Leander had a nightshift, Lenore and son spent a lot of time going to the movies. "My mother was a picture fan," Gene would recall. "My dad used to work nights. At least once a week, Mom would say, 'Okay! We're going to the movies!' She was enamored. I saw *Sign of the Cross* with Fredric March and Claudette Colbert … I never missed a Laurel and Hardy picture. Ever!"[11] His devotion to Stan and Ollie took a backseat, however, when Gene discovered the mystical world of *Chandu the Magician,* a popular radio show. He was immersed in Chandu for over a year, persuading his mother to switch her brand of soap, so he could mail in box-tops for assorted Chandu magic tricks.[12] After Gene's penchant for the supernatural miraculously vanished, Leander introduced his son to marvels of the *real* world.

"Dad loved the sand, the beach, the water," recalled Gene. "We'd go down there and he would teach me elementary acrobatics, handsprings, flips, which I took to very easily. The apple didn't fall far from the tree in that respect."[13] Gene loved being in the air. "For me, the trampoline was a marvelous thing," he admitted. "Jumping up and flipping. I became quite a show-off."[14] Aside from being a very fine athlete, Leander had a penchant for roller-skating and … ballroom dancing! "He loved to dance," said Gene. "I understand he was considered a local expert with the tango. So when I became interested in dancing myself, I had a very supportive father."[15]

It was Fred Astaire, however, that triggered Gene's passion for dance. As mentioned, Astaire's appearance in *Flying Down to Rio* (1933) fueled Gene's interest (with the support of his parents) in taking dance lessons. As Gene later put it, "In defense of my mother's hardwood floors—which I was scratching badly trying to emulate Mr. Astaire—I was enrolled in a class at the Miramar Hotel."[16] His instructor was Roy Randolph, known for his limber high kicks and fraternizing with the stars. Randolph staged and directed Saturday Matinee Kiddie Revues at the Fox-Wilshire Theatre in Beverly Hills—a venue that Eugene Berg ultimately missed out on.

"I liked going to class," said Gene, "but what I didn't realize was that I was required to practice what I'd learned—*every* day. My dad laid down a linoleum floor in the garage for me to practice on." When Gene slacked off practicing to engage in tree climbing, Leander gave an ultimatum, "No practice—no lessons!" His son's "career" was put on hold. It took over a year, but Gene got back on track thanks again to Fred Astaire. A family tragedy may have also contributed to Gene's taking his opportunities more seriously.

On May 22, 1934, Santa Monica's *Evening Outlook* reported that Leander and Lenore's infant daughter Nancy Lenore Berg had passed away. It was mentioned that Nancy was the sister of Eugene Berg. The notice indicated that a viewing would be held at the funeral parlor and memorial chapel of Todd & Leslie.[17] During his sobering sabbatical from dance classes, fourteen-year-old Eugene turned a new leaf.

***The Gay Divorcee* (1934) Astaire & Ginger Rogers (RKO)**

**1950 Golden Globe Awards - Fred Astaire & "Best Newcomer" Gene Nelson**

After seeing another Astaire musical (*The Gay Divorcee*) in the autumn of 1934, Gene informed his parents that he was eager to resume lessons ... and take them *seriously*. He enrolled at the Albright School of Dance. His instructor was a professional New York hoofer named Steve Granger. The first tap routine Gene tackled was "Doin' the New Low-Down," a 1928 hit originated by the celebrated African-American tap dancer, Bill "Bojangles" Robinson. "Steve knew all of Bill Robinson's routines," emphasized Gene. "It was fun to dance like the great 'Bojangles'."[18] To help pay for his dance lessons, Gene aligned himself with yet another celebrity. He worked for actor Robert Montgomery, exercising and feeding the popular MGM star's horses. Montgomery was an avid polo player. Teenager Gene Berg stuck to dancing.[19]

The confidence Gene acquired at Albright prompted him to entertain. "I teamed up with a fellow student named Ted Hansen," Gene recalled. "We got into a lot of flashy stuff like Toe Stands, Double Wings to Toe Stands, and a lot of challenge steps. We got pretty good and began doing free shows at the Veterans Hospital and the openings of markets where they used to do little promotional shows featuring local talent."[20] Gene confirmed, "We never got paid for anything."[21]

At Santa Monica High School (aka "Samohi") 1934-38, Gene faced yet another challenge. He was confronted by fellow students who believed that boys who took dance were "sissies." "I spent a lot of time defending myself," said Gene in 1989. "But that began to change when the 'macho boys' discovered I could be useful by performing at various school functions. Suddenly, I wasn't a 'sissy' anymore. They needed *me* to make *themselves* look good."[22] Gene and his pal Ted had the honor of entertaining U.S. Congressman John F. Dockweiler. After Dockweiler's speech at a school assembly where he promoted "staunch patriotism" and the need for military training camps, the Boy's Glee Club added a dash of levity. As the *Evening Outlook* reported, "Samohi's two ace tap dancers, Gene Berg and Ted Hansen, presented an amusing collegiate dance."[23] Two years later, Dockweiler made an unsuccessful attempt to run for Governor of California. Gene Berg, on the other hand, took an amazing step forward and was elected as both Head Cheer Leader, and Commissioner of Publications at Santa Monica High.

It was during his sophomore year at Samohi that Gene (as well as his pal Ted) enrolled in the most prestigious professional dance school in Hollywood: Fanchon & Marco. "I got heavily into acrobatic training and advanced tap and adagio work," Gene detailed. He recalled seeing Judy Garland, Ann Miller, and Rita Cansino (Hayworth) there. Hayworth assisted her father, teaching Spanish dancing. The school produced live prologues for the Paramount Theatre in downtown Los Angeles. They had a big chorus line called The Fanchonettes, similar to The Rockettes at Radio City Music Hall. At 15, as a top pupil, Gene (and Ted) participated in The

Fanchon & Marco Juvenile Revues at the Paramount—two-week stints, three times a year. This was his first professional job and paid $15 a week. "I learned a lot about show biz with them," Gene admitted. "But, by the time I was sixteen … my school work began to suffer greatly, and with the distinct threat of not graduating with my class." Leander and Lenore "pulled the plug," as Gene put it, so he could concentrate on his academic studies. "They were right, of course," said Gene. "And I graduated … barely."[24]

It wasn't only dance that distracted Gene from his scholastic studies. His tightrope and tumbling work made the news, as well as his *own* expertise in the art of news reporting. During his junior year, the City of Santa Monica honored Gene Berg by making him editor-for-a-day of the city's only daily newspaper *The Outlook*. The May 5th issue pictured Gene conferring with *Outlook* editor Samuel G. McClure. The following month, Gene made news again at Samohi's Honor Awards, where he received his varsity letter in track. To top things off, in June, Gene's photo was prominently displayed amongst a quartet of recently elected student officers. It was official … Eugene Berg was elected Yell Leader for his senior year.[25] He put together the largest cheerleading team in the history of Santa Monica High.

**Samohi Student Officers (1937): Smiling Eugene Berg – Yell Leader**

Despite the academic challenges, Gene waltzed away from Samohi after winning the Senior Waltz Contest. By then, Gene's Scandinavian roots found a new passion: ice-skating. In August 1938, only three months after graduation, he landed an audition for the *Hollywood Ice Revue* starring fellow Scandinavian, Sonja Henie. A three-time Olympic gold medalist, Henie was nicknamed "Pavlova of the Ice" due to her ability to spin endlessly while melding ballet into her performance. It made sense to eighteen-year-old Eugene Berg to follow suit. He abandoned tap for the time being, in order to master ballet and the art of the *pirouette* … on ice. "I studied with Bert Prival," recalled Gene. "He was marvelous to work with, and I treasure all the help he gave me."[26] Following two-hour ballet lessons with Prival, Gene would hit the ice. Despite numerous falls, bruises and scrapes, Gene enjoyed this transition. As he put it, "God! It was so wonderful!"[27]

# Chapter 2

# Life on Ice: 1938-1942

**Second Fiddle** (1939) – Gene Berg (insert)

While their son Eugene tripped the ice fantastic with Sonja Henie &
Co., Leander and Lenore moved to a bungalow on Pine Street. It
was located in the quaint, hilly part of Santa Monica, and not too far
from the ocean. Leander still worked at Douglas Aircraft. Lenore
was proprietor and baker for the Wee Bake Shop in West Los
Angeles.

Gene's career with Sonja began on senior class "ditch day" at
Samohi. He marched out of school with other rebel students,
borrowed a pair of ice skates and headed for the Polar Palace in
Hollywood. Ice-skating was different from anything he had ever

done. After his dayshift at a diner in Santa Monica, Gene began ice-skating every night. The manager of the Polar Palace was Bert Clark, an ex-hockey player from Canada. Prior to her screen debut, Sonja herself paid regular visits to the Polar Palace. When a hoped-for screen test with Paramount hadn't materialized, she was prepped to head back to Norway. It was Clark who encouraged Sonja to stage a show at the Polar Palace. Movie moguls then began bidding for her expensive talents. She rewarded Clark, hiring him to be her skate-in (stand-in) during rehearsals at 20th-Century Fox.[28]

Gene was aware that Bert Clark had his eye on him. Clark was also technical advisor for Sonja's ice shows. "Bert kept watching me all the time," said Gene. "I never took any lessons."[29] Clark suggested that Gene audition for the Sonja Henie *Hollywood Ice Revue*. He was hired on the spot. Gene Berg was a natural. During a three-month winter tour, he was in six routines that featured Sonja, and was paid $75 a week. "What a break!" Gene recalled. "I must say that my dance training put me way ahead of the game, and I progressed very rapidly."[30]

In March 1939, after touring the U.S. and Canada, Sonja was back in Hollywood to film *Second Fiddle* with Tyrone Power. The duo previously teamed for *Thin Ice* (1937), and were in a highly publicized romance offscreen. *Second Fiddle* was a breezy comedy that focused on the Hollywood publicity game. A pleasant Irving Berlin score included an Academy Award nomination for Best Song. Reviews were mixed, but fans helped fuel box-office returns. It was Hollywood poking fun at itself ... escapist fare ... a showcase for ice-skating ... and a star build-up for Henie.

Before shooting began, Gene joined Screen Actors Guild. He was assigned both skating and dancing scenes for the 20th Century Fox feature. His unique looks and talent are easy to spot in the musical-dance number "Back to Back." Advertising indicated that there were two numbers involving a chorus of skaters, including a rhumba that took six days to shoot. Unfortunately, these vignettes ended up on the cutting room floor.

While tensions mounted in Europe, the *Hollywood Ice Review* began a second whirlwind tour. Gene was allotted the honor of being the understudy for Henie's skating partner. He was also given some solo bits to perform.[31] When England and France declared war on Germany (September 3), cameras began to roll for *Everything Happens at Night*. The film's anti-Fascist stance reflected the times, but just barely. The implausible scenario included what audiences paid to see: Sonja hitting the ice. A climactic finish involving the Gestapo didn't compensate for the frivolity that surrounded a serious subject. It came as no surprise, however, when the film was banned in Nazi Germany. *Time* magazine aptly summed up, "Sonja Henie on blades is still the best part of her pictures." Once again, a skating scene involving Gene and other skaters, was cut before release. He was nowhere in sight.

Sonja Henie and Hitler. Yes, there were controversies surrounding the relationship between the skating star and *der Führer*. As a young amateur, she frequently performed in Germany, and was a personal favorite of Hitler. She gave command performances for Hitler, and also Mussolini, but claimed to have done so "grudgingly."[32] In 1936, after winning her third Olympic gold medal (and offering a Nazi salute along with other competitors) Sonja accepted an invitation to lunch with Adolf. He presented her with an autographed photo, personalized with a lengthy inscription. The Norwegian press chastised her for acquiescing to Hitler's request. Soon after the release of *Everything Happens at Night*, Sonja's homeland, the neutral, pacifist-leaning nation of Norway, was ill-prepared for Germany's swift military invasion. Biographer James Robert Parish indicated that over the ensuing years Henie's brief association with Hitler "would cause a lot of grief for her."[33]

<>>

While touring with Henie & Co., Gene resided with his parents. 1940's *Santa Monica Directory* indicated that Gene Berg supplemented his income as a skating instructor. Gene's ambition fueled another venture. "I found a little partner," he recalled. "We were the first exponents of jitterbug on ice. We developed a whole routine." The celebrity-ridden Cocoanut Grove provided artificial ice and a nine-week venue for their jitterbug act. The "little partner" Gene mentioned was sixteen-year-old Jo Ann Dean (who would later claim fame as the first Snow White at Disneyland). By July 1940, Gene and Jo Ann were jitterbugging on ice at the Orpheum Theatre in Los Angeles. *Billboard* reported "excellent business." The popular duo would team in various venues for two years.

**Gene with Jo Ann Dean**

Then came New York. Sonja Henie and business manager Arthur Wirtz produced the two-act *It Happens on Ice*. Rockefeller Center hosted the lavish production from October 1940 – June 1941. It clicked. Act I included "Wintertime" in which Gene Berg was designated as "The Show-Off" … echoes from his own childhood. The *New York Sun* noted, "They have engaged some of the most precocious boys and girls of the skating world to do their most extravagant capers. After the first few minutes, none of it seems quite real … ."[34] The reviewer, Richard Lockridge, concluded that the ice show was "pretty to look at for a while … beautiful, but pretty dumb." His main praise was reserved for comedian Joe Cook, a non-skater! SRO audiences thought otherwise, prompting an encore edition that ran from July 1941 to March 1942.

At the close of Act I, Gene and Jo Ann teamed with the entire company for "Don't Blow that Horn, Gabriel." It was situated in the program, in order for the cast to remove heavy makeup between acts – specifically: blackface, which was taking its time to lose favor with the public. African-Americans were denied entrance into most ice-rinks. However, one young black woman living in New York, Mabel Fairbanks, had the courage to push the envelope forward. After watching Sonja Henie on screen, Mabel was inspired to ice skate, honing her skill on the city's small winter ponds. The manager of Manhattan's Gay Blades Ice Rink, finally relented and allowed Mabel to skate during the last half-hour before closing. In time, people were calling her "The Sepia Sonja Henie." When Mabel attempted to contact Henie in hopes to be in one of her ice revues, Henie refused.[35] Mabel Fairbanks' skill and determination would one day garner her the honor of being the first African-American inducted into the U.S. Figure Skating Hall of Fame (1997).

*The Brooklyn Eagle* gave a nod to "Don't Blow that Horn, Gabriel" – calling it a "striking, Negro eye-number." The review pointed out the talents of Gene and Jo Ann, who were designated in this particular gig as: "In the Groove."[36] When it came to integrating black and white talent, Gene Berg would go against protocol and attempt to rectify the situation during WWII.

<<>>

*It Happens on Ice* had a weeklong stay in Chicago. Reporter Jack Gaver singled Gene Berg out as one of the "outstanding performers."[37] Gaver indicated that the ice spectacular "made a lot of money for Sonja Henie." Henie's passion for the almighty dollar was notorious. She was one of Hollywood's wealthiest women. Henie was currently touring in the *Sonja Henie Hollywood Ice Revue of 1941.* Sixty of her skating troupe went on strike after she lowered their wages from $75 a week, to $60.[38] She and manager Wirtz quelled this insurrection, demanding that the American Guild of Variety Artists suspend the entire company. Sonja, while receiving 50% of the entire gross of her ice shows, won the battle. In January 1942, *Variety* reported that the Henie revue grossed $1,054,000.

**It Happens on Ice (1940-42) Jo Ann, Gene**

Gene and Jo Ann averaged between $100-$200 a week during Rockefeller's encore edition of *It Happens on Ice.*[39] They starred in the revue's opening number, "Better Late Than Never" – with thirty-two supporting skaters. The duo also opened Act II with "Hielo Caliente" (hot ice), a salute to Pan-American relations, featuring the Conga, Rhumba and Tango. In another segment, Gene easily stood out while doing thirteen Arabian cartwheels in a row. This was done without hands! He was the first to perform this difficult maneuver on ice.[40] Overall, *It Happens on Ice* attracted more than 1.5 million viewers during its entire run.

The team of Gene and Jo Ann were non-stop, participating in an ice-revue at Hotel New Yorker's "Terrace Room." Gene opened the act with a free-style exhibition, before joining Jo Ann in a samba, then closing with a rhythmic routine to the popular Sammy Kaye hit, "Daddy!" The duo was not a romantic item. Fact was, Gene's head had been turned since the autumn of 1940, by a gal named Miriam.

During the initial run of *It Happens on Ice*, Gene spied an attractive young woman in the front row one evening. She had her eye on him. Smiles and winks were exchanged. He made a note of the beaver-skin coat she had on, and rushed out of the theater after the finale, but she was gone. A week later, she came backstage and introduced herself. Miriam Franklin. Barely a word passed between them before they heard "Places!" and the skaters took to the ice, where the flirtation by wink and smile resumed. Gene learned from cast members that Miriam had a big crush on him. The next day, he tried to telephone her at the 46th Street Theatre, where she was in rehearsals for *Panama Hattie*, starring Ethel Merman. He ended up leaving a note in her theater mailbox. A dinner date was arranged for the following evening. The night after that, Gene introduced Miriam to ice-skating. While in the rink, Gene kept her, as she put it, "on my feet and off my bottom." Coincidentally, fellow chorus girl Betsy Blair was dating another "Gene" with the last name Kelly. Kelly was being propelled toward stardom in *Pal Joey*. The two Genes would often arrive at the 46th Street Theatre at the same time. Miriam never forgot how the stage manager would yell into the dressing rooms: "Betsy! Miriam! Your Genes are here."[41]

**Boardwalk Boogie (1940) Will Bradley, Miriam and Gene**

The Berg-Franklin love-match began collaborating on dance routines. In December 1940, *Variety* reported that Gene and Miriam made their initial appearance as a team on film! An agent got them a gig for *Boardwalk Boogie* … a musical short designed for "Soundies" – a jukebox with a screen. Kids could insert a dime and watch the duo dance alongside trombonist Will Bradley and his Band … famous for their renditions of "Boogie-Woogie." Gene told the reporter from *Variety* that as soon as he taught Miriam to skate well enough, they would marry.[42] In the meantime, they enjoyed late evenings dancing at their favorite night spot, the Sports Bar at Hotel Belvedere. Gene resided at the Belvedere.

Miriam later reminisced, "Gene became as much of [my] group as I did his. We'd go sledding in Central Park. Then we'd have snowball fights. Gene was so much fun. You didn't want to dare him, because he'd try anything. I called him "Fearless Gene.""[43] By October 1941, Miriam's pals were calling *her*, "Legs." *P.M.* magazine singled Miriam out in the Broadway musical *Let's Face It!* "Long, leggy Miriam Franklin," they raved, "is the best chorus girl on Broadway." "Fearless Gene" and his sweetheart "Legs" were inseparable. "When we weren't on a date, we were talking on the phone," confirmed Miriam. "Both my parents liked Gene. It was sort of given that we'd get married." Gene also spent a lot of time playing the piano and serenading Miriam at her parents' apartment.[44] Miriam mentioned Gene's thoughtful and loving personality, and that he was always "as punctual as the sunrise."[45]

December 7, 1941. "We were just about to make our entrance for the matinee performance," recalled Gene, "when the news of Pearl Harbor flattened us."[46] It wasn't long before male members of *It Happens on Ice* were being drafted. Gene asked Miriam's father for her hand in marriage. His parents flew out from California to meet the bride-to-be … and offer their blessing. Columnist Dorothy Kilgallen chimed in with: "Broadway's first war marriage: Miriam Franklin, the captain of the chorus at *Let's Face It!* and Gene Berg of *It Happens on Ice*, will waltz down the aisle within the week." Gene later confessed that he proposed with an ultimatum: "Either you marry me now, or I can't guarantee whom I'll be seeing while I'm in the army, or that I'll be single when I get back." Miriam's comeback? "Let's get married right away!"[47] On December 22, they opted to go to City Hall. "We really weren't church goers," Miriam admitted. Her friend and fellow chorus girl June Allyson was maid-of-honor. Gene's skating partner Jo Ann Dean also joined the bridal party. When the newlyweds arrived at their hotel suite, a bottle of chilled champagne awaited them—a gift from Eve Arden.

**Newlyweds: December 22, 1941 (Photo by Bruno)**

"There wasn't much of a honeymoon," said Miriam. "We were both working." As Gene preferred not to be drafted, he enlisted in the Signal Corps at nearby Fort Monmouth, New Jersey. He was due to report there in March 1942. His assignment: Company Clerk. "God, I hated it!" Gene groaned.[48] "I was bored to death. All I had to do was sit on my butt and shuffle papers."[49] To the rescue came none other than … *ta-da* … Irving Berlin. In a matter of weeks, Gene Berg, in uniform, got off his butt and shuffled back to Broadway.

*This is the Army* (Broadway – 1942)

*This is the Army* (Warner Bros. – 1943)

# Chapter 3

# *This is the Army,* Pvt. Berg

Gene often reflected on his and Miriam's first Christmas together as husband and wife. Ten years later, in 1951, he put it into words, rather eloquently.

> *1941. It was a strange Christmas. Horrible for many people, but wonderful for us because we were young, married, and so terribly in love. Everywhere the grim tension of war was in the air and people were trying extra hard to enjoy themselves, to buy a little more than they had planned and to be a little nicer to their fellow man. You noticed it on the streets—people celebrating with the feeling that perhaps it was the last Christmas they'd know for years, perhaps forever.*[50]

The newlyweds had two months together, before Gene reported to Fort Monmouth. After basic training, Miriam was allowed to visit for a week. "For several seconds after I caught sight of him," she recalled, "I didn't recognize him. His hair had been G.I.-ed, he was thin as a needle, his cheeks were gaunt."[51] Gene's enlistment record for March 4, 1942, indicated that he was 5' 11" weighing in at 139 pounds. His disinterest in mathematics while at Santa Monica High came back to haunt him at this juncture. "It was because I couldn't do math that I flunked out in flying school during the war," said Gene, "and I wanted to fly more than anything else in the world."[52]

To keep boredom at bay, buck private Gene Berg found time to dance. "I had to do something to keep in shape and let off steam," he explained. "I had a portable radio and, in the evenings, I went to the recreation hall and danced."[53] He caught the eye of Pvt. First Class Irving Lazar, who asked Gene to entertain in a Camp Monmouth post show. Lazar, it turned out, was a New York agent, dealmaker, and future agent for the likes of Humphrey Bogart. "That was the best offer I'd had since I'd been there," said Gene. "The post show went great. What I didn't know was that Irving Berlin was in the audience … scouting for talent for an all-army show."[54] The composer liked what he saw. "A couple of days later," said Gene, "I came across a transfer report and my name was on it." He headed to Camp Upton (Long Island) to begin rehearsals, along with 365 other soldiers in a Special Services unit, for Irving Berlin's *This is the Army*. The musical would be a follow-up to Berlin's 1918 WWI all-army production *Yip Yip Yaphank*.

And Miriam? In many ways, she was paving the way for husband Gene's career in a *post-war* world. Miriam's own backstory underscores her ability to do exactly that. It all began when Miriam Louise Frankel quit school at the age of sixteen.

## Miriam Louise Frankel

"From early on I knew I wanted to be on the stage," wrote Miriam in her 2009 memoirs. "Both parents supported me from the get-go. They would have supported me if I wanted to be a garbage collector."[55] Miriam's earthly debut took place at Chicago's Edgewater Hospital on September 21, 1919.[56] Her father, Daniel Frankel, came from a large Jewish family in St. Louis. For a while he played around with vaudeville. Her mother, Miriam Bly Frankel, was born in Toronto. Being half-Jewish, half-Gentile was a real plus for Miriam Jr. "I … celebrated all the Christian holidays," she mused. "Then I got to be Jewish on the Jewish holidays … I got to be out of school more than the rest of the kids."

The Frankel family lived in various one-bedroom apartments. Miriam slept on the sofa. "We never had much money," she recalled, "but I was happy." When she was eight, her parents divorced, but remained on friendly terms. Her fascination with dance began when a tenant in the building placed a plaque on his door that read: "Ted Arkin – Tap Dancing." While Miriam couldn't afford lessons, Arkin eventually took pity and taught her a few steps. More good luck occurred when Mr. Frankel began producing nightclub shows. At rehearsals, Miriam would stand behind dancers and mirror their steps. Mother Miriam, as fate would have it, became head wardrobe lady for Chicago's Chez Paree, which featured stars like Sophie Tucker, Jimmy Durante and Helen Morgan. Showgirls loved pampering 12-year-old Miriam, teaching her the art of make-up and trying on costumes.

1935. Miriam and her mother relocated to New York City, where her parents reconciled. Mr. Frankel was now doing publicity on the east coast for photographer Tony Bruno—"Bruno of Hollywood."[57] Celebrities from stage, screen, and opera had posed for Bruno. Before long, Bruno photographed sixteen-year-old Miriam for advertising purposes. (In 1941, it would be Bruno who photographed newlyweds Gene and Miriam). Miriam opted to not go to high school. "I focused all my energy on my dancing career," she admitted. "My father found me the best tap dance school in the city. It was owned by Ernest Carlos, a really terrific black tap dance teacher. I was at the studio every day."[58] She wanted to be the next Eleanor Powell, her idol. "That was my goal," she said.[59]

Before long, Miriam was scouring the newspaper for audition notices. She got a few gigs, but was underage. She was often told "come back when you grow up."[60] She recalled guys in the chorus calling her "Jailbait." By January 1938, Miriam, no longer jailbait, was cast in *Let's Play Fair*, a satire on the upcoming World's Fair. It opened at showman Billy Rose's Casa Mañana. The *Times-Union* commented on the "bountiful parade of semi-nude dancers."[61] Famous stripper Sally Rand joined in the parade. Rose wanted the girls to wear G-strings. They rebelled, and were allowed to wear G-pants instead. "They were equivalent to bikini bottoms," Miriam clarified, "but were still racy for the time." Her dance partner for one number was future MGM star Van Johnson.

In the fall of 1938, Miriam Frankel made her Broadway debut in *Sing Out the News.* Her audition went so well, that she was asked to coach a "little blonde" in need of a dance routine for the tryout. Miriam detailed: "I was so thrilled about the prospect of being in a Broadway show I would have done anything. So, I took the 'little blonde' to a rehearsal hall to teach her something. ... She was chosen. It was her first Broadway show, too. Her name was June Allyson."

Gene Berg's marriage proposal in 1941 was not Miriam's first. During the run of *Sing Out the News,* she had a big crush on a cast member named Pete. "We got serious," she recalled, "we even discussed marriage. Then Pete surprised me one evening. He hemmed and hawed ... 'Miriam', he told me. 'I can't marry you.' 'Why not?' I wanted to know. 'Because you're Jewish.'"[62] She hadn't realized that being Jewish could have what she referred to as "a negative effect." After all, Miriam was surrounded by prominent, influential, Jewish talent in theater arts.

During *Sing Out the News* Miriam was encouraged to change her last name. She considered using her mother's maiden name Bly, but opted to simply turn Frankel into Franklin. The newly christened Miriam Franklin wrapped up the year in two more Broadway shows, the musical-comedy *Yokel Boy* starring Judy Canova, and composer Jerome Kern's *Very Warm for May.* The latter, directed by Vincent Minnelli, only lasted 59 performances, but Miriam was proud to have been in a Jerome Kern musical, alongside her good friend June Allyson and the witty Eve Arden. One nine-year-old in the audience was so inspired that he determined to have a career in musical theater—the legendary Stephen Sondheim.

The year 1940 was another turning point for Miriam. Her skill with choreography kept turning heads. Upon joining Cole Porter's *Panama Hattie,* starring Ethel Merman and Betty Hutton, Miriam was assigned by choreographer Bob Alton to be line captain. She was in charge of chorus rehearsals. "Alton," Miriam later confirmed, "was the biggest influence on me becoming a choreographer." To top things off, glamour shots of Miriam Franklin were being used for advertising the popular skin cream Noxzema. Miriam also nudged her friend June to try out as Betty Hutton's understudy. Thanks to Miriam, June got to fill in one evening for Hutton. June so impressed a rep from producer George Abbott's office, that she was hired for the musical *Best Foot Forward.* MGM liked what they saw and put her in the film version. As Miriam summed up, "The rest is June Allyson history!"

Miriam Louise Frankel was an essential ingredient in the "history" of Gene Nelson. Gene himself acknowledged, "It was Miriam who got me back on track with dancing." In February 1943, Gene's company from *This is the Army* would head to Hollywood to take a final bow, and make a film version. After filming wrapped at Warner Bros., that was the end of *This is the Army.* Then, in a complete about-turn, half the troops were retained. Pvt. Gene Berg's dancing feet were about to circumnavigate the globe for *two more* years in …

## *This is the Army*

"I learned more about theater and show business in those two years," Gene emphasized. "It would have taken twelve years at home under normal conditions to accumulate that much experience. Hell, we performed in the rain, in thunder and lightning, under the wildest conditions you could ever imagine."[63] The original production had opened at the Broadway Theatre on July 4, 1942. "It was an instant smash," said Gene. "SRO for six months at the Broadway and then we went on a national tour. We traveled by train and paraded from the train station to the theater with full marching band in every city. The biggest thrill of the tour happened in Washington D.C. … FDR and Eleanor came to a special matinee performance." That evening the cast was invited by President Roosevelt to a late supper at the White House. "We were all *individually* introduced to him," Gene underscored. "I'll never forget it."[64] FDR was up until 1:30am shaking hands with the entire company.

Intended as a morale-booster, *This is the Army*, a two-act musical revue, paid tribute to each branch of the armed services. In her 2021 book *God Bless America – Tin Pan Alley Goes to War*, author Kathleen Smith wagered that army life in the Berlin musical had all appearances of a summer camp vacation. There were no battle scenes, no deaths, no destruction. Gene Berg appeared in several sequences, occasionally donning feminine attire (as did Burl Ives).

**Pvt. Berg on screen (1943)** *This is the Army* **(WB)**

While filming in Hollywood, Gene's unit camped near Warner Bros., marching daily, in formation, to the sound stages. Stars recruited for the film's subplot, included George Murphy, Joan Leslie, Ronald Reagan, Rosemary DeCamp, Una Merkel, and an uncredited Dan Dailey. Irving Berlin, world heavyweight champ Joe Louis, and Kate Smith played themselves. Smith's iconic technicolor rendition of "God Bless America" was a highlight. Warner Bros. opted to *include* battle scenes, death and destruction. It also opted for a reprise of Berlin's 1918 song "Mandy" – which had the misfortune of being performed in "blackface." Although his earlier works included racial stereotypes, Berlin himself had composed the first anti-lynching song "Supper Time" in 1933. It was sung by Ethel Waters in the Broadway revue *As Thousands Cheer.*

Gene indicated that for him, the real show-stopper was "What the Well-Dressed Man in Harlem Will Wear"—performed by an all-black contingent. "They were some of the greatest hoofers around," said Gene, "and never failed to stop the show cold. It was a barn-burner, let me tell you!"[65] Gene's opinion is easily understood upon viewing the Warner Bros. film. All profits ($10 million) from the 1942 Broadway production as well as the 1943 film version, which won an Academy Award for Best Score, were donated to the Army Emergency Relief Fund, which in turn went to families of those who died in battle.[66]

No doubt the biggest thrill for Gene while filming in Hollywood, was an encounter with his idol Fred Astaire. Fred was at RKO rehearsing a number for *The Sky's the Limit* (1943). "I was in uniform, and I snuck onto the lot," Gene confessed. "It wasn't hard in uniform. No one would dare question a serviceman in those days." As Gene roamed the sound stages, he heard the sound of taps. Gene recalled ...

> *I quietly moved around the bandstand and there he was, the King, himself. A towel around the neck, shirt open at the collar, and the traditional necktie around his waist as a belt. ... I can't describe my feelings, except that I suddenly felt I was stealing something very valuable.*[67]

Astaire looked up, noticed the young man in uniform, and greeted him warmly. "He graciously interrupted his rehearsal to chat with me for a few minutes," Gene remembered. "I told him how I loved all his routines." Gene then asked Astaire how he came up with all those "wild ideas of using furniture, golf clubs, whatever was handy" while dancing. Astaire answered with a modest reply, "I don't know

... you don't know if these things will work until you try them" ... words that would echo in Gene's head for decades to come.

After Hollywood, *This is the Army* headed to England. Gene's journalism skills from Samohi paid off when recalling his time overseas. In 1989, Gene was asked to detail his global WWII experiences. He put pencil to paper, graciously obliging with a vivid and compelling overview, including the following excerpt ....

> *We opened at the Palladium Theatre in London in November 1943. We performed for the Queen of England ... General Eisenhower ... and a load of other dignitaries, both military and civilian. Then off to tour the provinces— Scotland, Midlands, and Ireland. Our last stop before leaving the British Isles was Liverpool, where we boarded a troop ship bound for Italy by the way of Algiers.*

While in London, amid Nazi air-raids, Gene fell while leaping over a table during a performance. He severely wrenched both his knee and ankle. Pvt. Berg was told that he might never walk again. After wearing a cast for several weeks, he (no surprise here) came through .... *dancing*. In Algiers the show was limited to nine men. Sergeant and stage manager Alan Anderson appointed Berg as team captain. In 2004, Anderson recalled, "Gene was a very strong and athletic dancer, very handsome and well liked. He chose the eight other men."[68] While Berlin broke the color barrier in the armed forces, insisting that all men travel and bunk together, Gene created the only *truly* integrated show during the tour. He selected three black dancers, allowing human emotions and talent *on stage* to be a visual in black and white. Segregation of U.S. armed forces would be abolished after President Truman signed an executive order in July 1948.[69] Nonetheless, after returning home to partake in the freedoms for which they had fought, black WWII veterans were prime targets for assault, lynchings, and police brutality.[70]

**Santa Maria, Italy (1944) Gene – third from left**

April 1944 found Gene & Co. in full force opening at the San Carlo Opera in Naples—a six-month venue. Gene detailed …

*We headed north and east, getting closer to the front-line action. Some camps had no theaters—just big stage platforms, and the troops sat on the hillsides. Santa Maria, Foggia, Bari, and then we followed the Fifth Army into Rome as they chased the Germans out. Well, from there we headed east to Egypt, Iran, India. God, Iran was the pits. When we got there in September, it was around a hundred and twenty-five degrees. ... Then to the South Pacific. You got to remember that we were like a traveling circus.*

**South Pacific – Island of Tinian (1945) – Gene far right**

The vast Pacific Theater welcomed them in New Guinea in December 1944. The men had many responsibilities other than performing. Gene was assistant stage electrician, and volunteered for various duties. As he put it …

*I learned to operate the steam winch to unload our show onto trucks at each port o' call. I got to like that a lot—it was fun, and I got damn good at it. We'd do the show, tear it down, load everything back on the trucks, and head back to the boat. … Even if it was outdoors, we had to make it look just like Broadway for those guys. We thought at first, these combat guys would resent us, but not so. Some of them would come up and just want to touch us. You know what I mean? They were so glad to be there watching something that brought them closer to home. Our show was a jewel in the night.*

After New Guinea, the troop (boarding a smaller vessel) sailed toward the island of Manus. While performing on Manus, they suddenly heard gunshots. Japanese snipers had been watching the show while hiding in the surrounding trees! Somehow, Gene and Co. managed to get back to their ship. A few days later, Gene came to the rescue at a crucial moment. Sgt. Robert Sidney (well-known choreographer) remembered:

> *One afternoon at sea, someone inadvertently threw a cigarette, which landed on a tarp that covered the aft part of the ship, and started a fire. Gene Nelson happened to be sunning himself. He sprang into action  immediately. We don't know how he did it, but he got the tarp in one hand,  ripped it across the ship and dived into the ocean with the flaming tarp in  his hand. He really saved our lives, even though he could have killed  himself. But Gene was like that. We used to call him The All-American Boy Scout.*[71]

September 2, 1945. Where was fearless Gene on that memorable day?

> *We were on Guam when the war ended. A few more islands and many more shows later, we finished the tour in Honolulu ... Then it was all over—back to the States and discharge. ... Total performances—1,238. Grand total attendance—2,468,005 armed forces and civilian. God, I wouldn't do it again for a million dollars. But I wouldn't take a million dollars for that experience.*[72]

After the final performance in Honolulu (October 22, 1945), Irving Berlin walked to stage center and stated, "I hope to God I'll never have to write another war song."[73] He didn't. However, the Military-Industrial complex that President Dwight Eisenhower would warn the country about, was gaining momentum. The "large arms industry" and "power of money," as Eisenhower indicated, merged with an "immense military establishment" to fuel the U.S. war machine for decades to come.

# Chapter 4

# Hooray for Hollywood?

"On that wonderful day when he came home in 1945," recalled Miriam, "he walked in, looked around and said, 'I've been here a hundred times in my dreams. It's *really* home.'"[74] She and Gene easily reconnected, even though they were sharing an apartment with her mother. Career-wise, Gene wasn't sure what he was going to do.

Miriam had appeared in film musicals, credited as "Miriam Franklin," and was an assistant dance director at Paramount. She dubbed tap sounds for Betty Hutton, Dorothy Lamour, Bing Crosby, Bob Hope, and Ginger Rogers. On screen, Miriam and Canadian dancer Johnny Coy stood out in the 1945 release *Duffy's Tavern*, dancing in a clever scenario about love during war time. She had to admit, "This was an exciting time for me!" Once Gene returned from the service, however, Miriam shifted her priorities. "Back *then*," she emphasized, "a wife was expected to focus on her husband's career. Not that I minded. Nothing thrilled me more than seeing my husband succeed."[75] Hollywood actor-turned-agent John Darrow, an acquaintance of Miriam, was familiar with Gene's talent. Darrow handled the likes of Gene Kelly, June Allyson, Van Johnson and MGM director/choreographer Charles Walters (Darrow's love interest and companion). In early 1946, Darrow called the Berg residence. "I met him," said Gene, "and he asked if I'd audition for him. I did, and he liked what he saw. I signed with him."[76]

Darrow thought Gene would have a good chance at Twentieth Century-Fox. The studio had no dancing male leads to play opposite Betty Grable and June Haver. Darrow arranged a screen test. "I was over-anxious, nervous, tied-up by tension," recalled Gene.[77] He and

Miriam rehearsed a dramatic scene, and choreographed a dance number. She accompanied him to Fox studio. "I was as nervous as Gene," said Miriam. Regardless of nerves, Fox was impressed and signed Gene Berg to a stock contract (March 1946). There remained one little problem … his name.[78] Gene put it this way, "One of the executives, a little Jewish man, rather ironically decided my Swedish name, Berg, was 'too Jewish' and ordered it be changed. I submitted a few suggestions, among which was the last name of Nelson, my mother's maiden name. They liked it, and my new identity began— Eugene Leander Berg became Gene Nelson."[79] While studio executives didn't ask him to lie about his age (26), Gene's youthful looks would soon be assessed as being …  problematic.

20th Century-Fox. As a contract player, Gene eagerly took advantage of the studio's training program which included acting, deportment, and other camera-ready skills. One day, while dancing solo in a rehearsal hall, he caught someone's eye. "June Haver stuck her head in the door and watched," recalled Gene. "I wasn't rehearsing anything in particular, just trying new combinations and rhythms and tricks—getting ready for whatever. After a while she left."[80] "Whatever" turned out to be a role in June's upcoming film-musical *I Wonder Who's Kissing Her Now.* Haver had previously seen Gene perform at the Fox Studio Club's annual bash at the Cocoanut Grove (May 1946). The twenty-year-old had her eye on him ever since. She asked to see Gene's screen test, then made persistent demands for Gene to be her dance partner in three production numbers. June told columnist Ida Zeitlin, "He'll be the Gene Kelly of the 20th lot, you watch—."[81] After completing *I Wonder Who's Kissing Her Now*, June rhapsodized, "I'm prouder of having had a hand in 'discovering' Gene than of almost anything I've ever done."[82] Gene later acknowledged, "June was a very lovely, kind girl, and I'll always be grateful. … I felt things were really moving along for me."[83]

**Choreographer Hermes Pan directs Gene and June – Fox's new "Fred and Ginger" (Summer 1946)**

Filming began mid-July 1946. The director was Lloyd Bacon, who had teamed with Busby Berkeley for musical classics like *42nd Street*. Gene's enthusiasm was amplified when he learned that choreographer Hermes Pan, who had worked so closely with Fred Astaire, was assigned to *I Wonder Who's Kissing Her Now*. The turn-of-the-century plot was a mostly fictionalized biography of Broadway composer/troubadour Joseph Howard, who in real-life chalked up nine marriages.[84] On screen, Joe wasn't allowed any. This nostalgic peek into the past begins with Joe (Mark Stevens) bidding adieu to his adopted teenaged sister Katie (Haver), to tour with a lovely songstress named Lulu. When Katie shows up again, Lulu is not happy. Joe and Katie decide to form their own act. The predictable, tongue-in-cheek scenario ends with a fade-out kiss between, as you may have guessed, Joe and Katie. "As usual," sums up film historian Leonard Maltin, "music is better than script."[85] The real surprise (for 1947 audiences) was the love-duet "Good-bye, My Lady Love," where a dark-skinned Haver flirtatiously charms her white-skinned suitor (Stevens). In 2017 novelist/biographer Jacqueline T. Lynch commented, "I have to smile, wondering if Hollywood inadvertently pulled a fast one on the racists who were so careful to avoid such cozy interracial images."[86]

More interesting than the plot, was the legal action that took place *after* the film was released. Composer Harold Orlob took Joseph Howard to court, claiming that *he* wrote the title song. Fox had promoted the song as Howard's "most famous tune." Orlob won the case. Audiences, nevertheless, were enthusiastic. *I Wonder Who's Kissing Her Now* was among *Variety*'s "Top Grossers of 1947"— raking in $3,000,200.[87]

Gene, as dancer Tommy Yale, shows up in the last 30 minutes. We hear him crooning "What's the Use of Dreaming?" before facing the camera to say his only three lines in the film. Gene next shows up during Haver's beautifully choreographed "Glow-Worm," exiting center-stage with a series of mesmerizing leaps and twirls. The grand finale consists of three sequences. Gene, in a white wig and French tailcoat, does a brief minuet with a coquettish Madame Du Barry (Haver). Donning a Cossack uniform, he leaps into Russian squats with high kicks until Haver, as Catherine the Great, threatens to send him to Siberia. Haver next emerges as turn-of-the-century icon, Lillian Russell. Enter President Teddy Roosevelt, who offers his hand for a waltz. An arduous young gent (Nelson) taps Teddy on the shoulder, and cuts in. Lillian doesn't mind at all. An amusing ending that, as one critic put it, "sent folks away whistling, humming, and happy."[88]

***I Wonder Who's Kissing Her Now*** (1947) **Gene with June Haver**
**(20th Century-Fox)**

While Gene easily outshines the terpsichorean skill of the entire
cast, he wasn't allowed the opportunity for a revealing solo moment.

Perhaps studio head Darryl Zanuck wanted Haver to hold center stage. According to one biographer, Hermes Pan "spoke repeatedly of how much he enjoyed working with June Haver and Gene Nelson and predicted that they would become the successors of Fred Astaire and Ginger Rogers, a prophecy that unfortunately never materialized."[89]

**Gene in trailer for *Miracle on 34th Street* (1947) (20th Century-Fox)**

After filming was complete, Gene was asked to do a promotional trailer for Fox Studio's *Miracle on 34th Street* (1947). He played one of several enthusiastic studio executives who preview the film. The studio head (an obvious take on Zanuck) hollers that he finds the picture "Groovy!" Nelson and the others reply, "Yes, Mr. Schaffer!" Gene was then told by the casting office to see writer/producer Lamar Trotti about playing a burlesque song-and-dance man opposite Betty Grable in *Mother Wore Tights* (1947). Co-staring with Grable would be a godsend. Trotti took one look at Gene and started to laugh. "I had no idea why," Gene recalled. "Then he apologized and told me, 'We have no part for Betty Grable's son!' I was twenty-six years old, and I looked about eighteen. They hired Dan Dailey for the role."[90] Dailey, just returned from the army, had done films for MGM. At this point in his so-called film career, Gene had been pigeonholed as being too youthful. He must have wondered,

"What next?" But more likely, Gene Nelson was consumed with the responsibilities of … fatherhood. A baby was on its way!

In 2009, Miriam reminisced, "Nine months passed quickly. As the delivery date drew closer, June Haver threw me a baby shower."[91] On May 9, 1947, Miriam awoke with labor pains. It was still dark outside. Gene shot out of bed to bring the car in front of their apartment. Miriam hopped in and they sped off. "I was petrified," she said. "I might have the baby in the car and 'Fearless Gene' would attempt to cut the cord." Well, *that* didn't happen. Alan Christopher Berg was born hours later weighing in at seven pounds, ten ounces, and twenty-one inches long.[92]

As a father, Gene was a natural. He and Christopher became pals and playmates. Before Chris turned one, however, his dad's career at Fox was one disappointment after another. The studio relegated Gene to uncredited bit parts. While the films were major releases, Gene Nelson's participation went unnoticed. *Gentleman's Agreement*, an exposé on antisemitism, won the Academy Award for Best Picture of 1947. Halfway into the film, Gene shows up at a hotel desk where star Gregory Peck makes an inquiry. Peck heads to the dining room where he joins John Garfield and Celeste Holm. Gene and his friend (Robert Karnes) are about to sit at an adjoining table, when Karnes targets Garfield, calling him a "Yid." The two start to tussle until Gene apologizes for his pal, "Sorry! He's terrible when he gets all tanked up!" Gene escorts the troublemaker out of the dining room, scolding him with, "What's the matter with you anyway?" Gene holds his own in this brief encounter with the tension it demands. For a dash of irony, Peck's character changes his name from Green to Greenberg, to make it sound more Jewish. Perhaps if Gene had waited to sign with Fox in 1947, we would know him today as "Gene Berg."

***Gentleman's Agreement*** **(1947) Gregory Peck, Celeste Holm, John Garfield, Gene, Robert Karnes (20th Century-Fox)**

***The Walls of Jericho*** **(1948) Gene peeks over the shoulder of prosecutor Art Baker (20th Century-Fox)**

In the Fall of 1947, Gene was barely a ripple in producer Lamar Trotti's meandering *The Walls of Jericho*. During the film's climactic trial, Trotti cast Nelson as an assistant prosecutor with no lines. After that, MGM let Gene know that producer Arthur Freed was considering him to play opposite Judy Garland for the musical *Easter Parade*. Due to a broken ankle, Gene Kelly had been forced to drop out. As fate would have it, Gene's idol, Fred Astaire, twenty-three years older than Judy, was persuaded to come out of retirement to woo her on screen.[93]

***Apartment for Peggy*** **(1948) Edmund Gwenn, Jeanne Crain, William Holden, Randy Stuart, Gene (20th Century-Fox)**

Gene was being considered to play opposite Jeanne Crain in director George Seaton's engaging *Apartment for Peggy* (1948).[94] He ended up being seen for a total of 25 seconds. Fox decided on William Holden—they "needed a name" to carry the picture. The film advocated "not holding the book too closely"—but standing back to see the "bigger picture." Gene Nelson got the message, and began distancing himself from Hollywood. When a new opportunity came his way, he recognized it and made the necessary … transition. Soon after Gene's swansong for Fox was released, he was in a *bona fide* career changer co-starring Carol Channing … on Broadway.

Actor William Eythe bought rights to the musical revue *Lend an Ear*. Like Nelson, Eythe's career at 20th Century-Fox had been terminated. In 2001, author William J. Mann detailed: "Eythe defied Code-era tradition by living openly with another man, Lon McCallister. Poised on the brink of stardom, Eythe was suddenly yanked back. Studio chief Darryl Zanuck … 'wasn't too happy'

about the Eythe-McCallister friendship. Zanuck insisted the pair not be seen in public, and when they defied him, he released Eythe from his contract."[95] Eythe's attempt at marriage (1947) was short-lived. McCallister was also booted from Fox. He co-starred with June Haver in his final film for the studio, *Scudda Hoo! Scudda Hay!* (1948). With a nudge from June, no doubt, Lon promoted Gene to be in *Lend an Ear*.

As producer (and cast member) Eythe opted not to rely on star names, but punch through with new and fresh personalities like Gene Nelson and Carol Channing. Curiously, thirteen of the twenty-one cast members in *Lend an Ear* had been fired from various studios.[96] By May 1948, *Lend an Ear* was in rehearsal. Things really got underway once Gower Champion joined in with his inventive choreography.[97] As Channing later commented, Champion "was a man hell-bent for success. I was completely comfortable with his despotism."[98] So was Gene. He and Gower became fast friends.

Opening at Hollywood's Las Palmas Theatre on June 16, 1948, *Lend an Ear* offered Gene four stand-out numbers. *Los Angeles Daily News* praised: "Nelson has a tough realism, especially in his 'Who Hit Me' number." The sexy steam generated from "Who Hit Me?" placed Nelson, along with Channing and Eythe, as the top attractions. Celebrity-filled SRO crowds attended Las Palmas night after night. Within a matter of weeks Eythe called the company on stage to announce that Broadway producer Josh Logan was buying the show for $30,000. *Lend an Ear* was going to Broadway that fall.

**1948 – Lon McCallister, Dorothy Babb, William Eythe**

On November 10, 1948, Gene flew from Los Angeles to New York. Alone. In more ways than one. As far as Miriam was concerned, Gene's relationship with one of his co-players had crossed the line. She reflected rather succinctly on the situation in her autobiography:

> *... a few chinks had begun to develop in our marriage. I don't want to sound like I'm defending Gene, but you can't imagine the kind of pressure women  place on a young, athletic, attractive star to stray. One woman even had the audacity to bring a pie to our home. Gene was already kind of vulnerable  because he had an eye for women. I certainly wasn't the kind of wife to keep  her husband on a leash. My motto was "Look, but don't touch." But Gene developed a relationship with a dancer from Lend an Ear that crossed over  my boundaries of acceptability. We separated. Then Gene went to Broadway.*[99]

Prior to Gene's flight to New York, columnist Dorothy Kilgallen blabbed about the "Hollywood scenario going on backstage" in *Lend an Ear*, namely the affair between Gene and dancer Dorothy Babb.[100] Coincidentally, Babb was the former wife of Miriam's co-star from *Duffy's Tavern*, Johnny Coy. Their 1946 marriage spelled trouble from the beginning. A divorce. A reconciliation. Another divorce. By the time *Lend an Ear* opened at Broadway's National Theater (December 16), Gene made a plea to Miriam that they reconcile. She opted to fly to New York, leaving Chris in the care of her mother. "Gene and I decided to make a go of it," she recalled. "We found an apartment. I flew back to California to get Chris. ... Our family was together again. I loved being back in New York. We lived happily like that for most of that year [1949]."[101]

On January 23, 1949, Gene made his television debut on Ed Sullivan's *Toast of the Town*, where he and cast members did routines from *Lend an Ear*. The show transferred to the Broadhurst Theatre,

and played to capacity audiences. Critics invariably singled
Channing and Nelson out for praise. Drama critic Robert Garland
"couldn't stop raving" about Gene's "show-stopping terpsichorean
talents." AP critic Mark Barron underscored, "The cast is mainly
unknown to Broadway. Carol Channing and Gene Nelson head the
company … they will not be unknown for long."[102] *Billboard*
summed things up saying, "Nelson's dancing is about the most
startling stuff on feet seen yet. A dancer who will be sought by every
musical producer in the book."[103]

*Lend an Ear* (1948-49) **with Yvonne Adair in the steamy "Who Hit
Me?"**

<\>>

Finally. From a distance of 2,500 miles, Hollywood saw Gene Nelson in a new light. His agent was contacted by Warner Brothers. The studio wanted Gene to test for the musical *The Daughter of Rosie O'Grady*. Filming would begin in August. Gene clarified in 1989, "What I didn't know was that June Haver was starring … and she had told Bill Jacobs, the producer, that she wanted to dance with me in the picture. That's how the offer came about."[104] Or, as Hedda Hopper put it, "Bill Eythe gave Gene Nelson leave of absence from *Lend an Ear*, so June Haver could have him in *Daughter of Rosie O'Grady*." It was understood that Nelson would return to Broadway in eight weeks. By the time filming wrapped, however, Warner Bros. signed him to a contract. The Great White Way didn't let go of Gene Nelson easily. In 1949, Gene, along with Carol Channing and Julie Harris, were among the recipients of Broadway's annual Theater World Awards, joining previous honorees such as Patricia Neal, Burt Lancaster, Judy Holliday, and Marlon Brando.

*Tea for Two* (1950) Doris and Gene dance to "No, No, Nanette" (WB)

*The Daughter of Rosie O'Grady* (1950) with June Haver (WB)

# Chapter 5

# At Warner Brothers - Dancing 37-Miles a Day

A Warner Bros. contract enabled Gene to buy a home on Morningside Drive in Burbank. The studio itself was in Burbank. As Miriam was determined to go back to work, her mother moved in. Three-year old Chris and his "Nana" looked after each other, while his parents hit the soundstages.

Warner Bros. dance director LeRoy Prinz placed Miriam as head choreographer *after* she agreed to dance in Gene's first picture. She revealed that Gene had one complaint at this juncture. "His only objection," she said, "is that he feels I, too, should be in the limelight. He dreams of us as dancing partners."[105] *The Daughter of Rosie O'Grady* allowed them to do just that—if only briefly. The diverting opening number "A Farm Off Old Broadway" also allowed Gene to kiss Miriam on the cheek before his breathtaking forward-flip onto a haystack! The 1890's musical-romance gave Gene the opportunity to *stand out*. As one critic put it,

> *For this observer the performance of the tall, blonde Nelson, rising young dancer who scored on Broadway ... is one of the shows chief assets. Not only does he dance beautifully, but he has an unusually ingratiating screen personality. It won't be surprising if he becomes one of the screen's favorite dancing stars before long.*[106]

***The Daughter of Rosie O'Grady*** **– Gene and Miriam dance to "A Farm Off Old Broadway" (WB)**

Set in 1898, the story about an ex-vaudevillian with three daughters, focused on June Haver's attempt to defy papa and go on stage. As the determined rebel, Haver, on loan-out from Fox, offers a charming portrayal for a predictable scenario. The added plus of teenager Debbie Reynolds as June's spunky kid sister (one review called her a "cute little brat") guarantees some chuckles amid all the horn-locking. Director David Butler advised Debbie *not* to act, just be herself. It worked. Gene, billed fifth in the star line-up, played baritone Gordon MacRae's best chum (and rival for June). Gene's casual ease as an actor was part of his appeal, along with the bonus of his own mellow baritone for the 1900 hit, "Ma Blushin' Rosie." Gene and June team for a waltz, a ragtime tap-dance, and a winter finale in which Gene simulates ice-skating. Gene later qualified, "In those days LeRoy Prinz really held domain over all musical numbers. The billing was always: "Musical numbers staged and directed by LeRoy Prinz" – which was *not* true. I created all the choreography for my numbers. Prinz had great ideas. I worked closely with him."[107]

Audiences found *The Daughter of Rosie O'Grady* a tuneful, breezy affair. Was Warner Bros. pleased with Gene "Tappy Toes" Nelson (as the film's preview christened him)? Studio executives had six weeks to pick up his option for another year. It didn't take long. After Russell Downing, an executive for Radio City Music Hall witnessed a private showing of … *Rosie O'Grady*, he told Warner Bros., "You have one of the greatest dancers of many years in this picture. We would like to have him on our stage if you will lend him to us."[108] This was a reverse procedure, as it was usually *the studio* that asked Downing to feature their stars on stage. Gene flew in from Burbank in early February to perform at Radio City with an exciting interpretation of "St. Louis Blues." *Variety* zeroed in on his "neat, individual style" and the striking ballet influence in his leaps and turns.

Upon completing … *Rosie O'Grady*, Gene and Miriam had the good fortune to take a vacation. Along with son Chris (in cowboy boots), they drove up to Oregon, before spending a few weeks at scenic June Lake in the Sierra Nevada. They rented a cabin, did a lot of fishing and outdoor cooking. Gene and Chris doted on each other. *Life* magazine captured father and son for their popular "Speaking of Pictures" series. A ten-photo spread caught Gene leaping all around Chris's crib at bedtime. With a fee-fi-fo-fum, it was *Gene and the Beanstalk* until Chris laughed himself to sleep.[109]

**1949 – Miriam, Chris, Gene in New York**

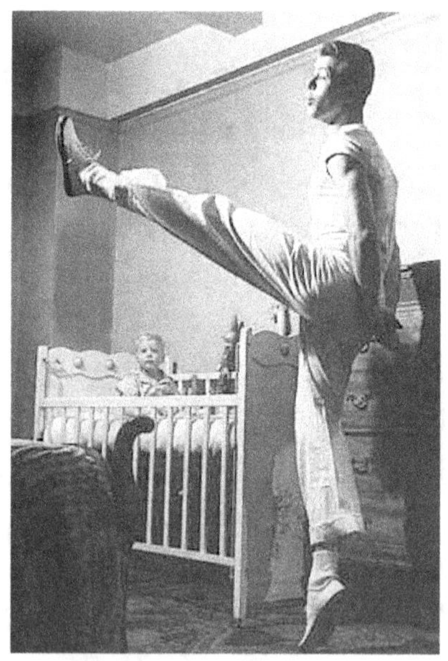

**Bedtime with *Gene and the Beanstalk***

Late March, 1950. Enter Doris Day. She and Gene would co-star in four films at Warner Bros. In her teens, Day had appeared in tap-dance reviews in her hometown of Cincinnati. When she was fifteen

(1937), her mother took her to Hollywood where Doris, like Gene, enrolled in the aforementioned Fanchon & Marco Studios. After a month, she returned to Cincinnati to prepare for a permanent move to Los Angeles. Unfortunately, a car accident left Doris with a fractured leg. She was told that dancing was out of the question. While on crutches, she took up singing. Her unique and appealing voice would bring her back to Hollywood a decade later. It wasn't until Gene and Miriam's encouragement in 1950, that Doris gave dancing a second try. She regained her confidence.

"When *Tea for Two* came along," said Day, "I was asked if I would like to take a crack at some tap routines with Gene Nelson. In a week and a half of rehearsals, going for eight hours every day, I've picked up the dancing that I never thought could be mine again. I'm in the groove once more, rarin' to go!"[110] Gene quipped, "She just about wore me out!"[111] Miriam indicated that Doris was quite a "daredevil." She watched Doris climb onto the roof, before diving into her swimming pool![112] "I thought Doris and Gene made a good dance couple," mused Miriam, "because she *also* was fearless."[113] Typical of fearless Gene, while working with Doris he decided to gauge exactly how many miles a day he danced. He strapped a pedometer to his ankle one day and logged in 37 miles.[114]

*Tea for Two* was a spinoff of the 1924 Broadway hit *No, No, Nanette*. The crux of the plot had Nanette (Day) betting her rich uncle (S.Z. Sakall) that she could go 48 hours without saying "yes" to anything. A cash reward of $25,000 would allow Nanette the funds to stage a musical for her two-timing boyfriend (Billy De Wolfe). A series of comical complexities raise their heads. Turns out that uncle lost all his dough in the stock market. Not to worry. Nanette's best pal (the always welcome Eve Arden) charms her way into the solvent pockets of a wealthy attorney. The direction by David Butler captures the mellow blend of vocals by Day and Gordon MacRae, along with the natural simpatico of Gene and Doris in their dance numbers. Despite an overdose of antics by Sakall and De Wolfe, it all added up to what *Variety* described as "the type of beguiling musical nonsense that practically always finds a ready reception." The film earned $3,652,000 at the box-office worldwide, confirming *Variety*'s opinion.

***Tea for Two*** **(1950) Doris and Gene (WB)**

The real dazzlers for cinemagoers were Gene's jungle gyrations to "Crazy Rhythm" atop a large tropical drum, and later on, tapping his way not only up and down a staircase—but along the banister! *New York Post* raved, "Gene Nelson leaps, taps and twirls with the best of them. His flip, clearly beyond the call of dancer's duty is an indication of rare coordination not often found in tall handsome young men."[115] *Film Bulletin* summed up, "The talented, personable Gene Nelson triumphs in three dance routines."[116] *Motion Picture Daily* confirmed, "Gene Nelson is no less than sensational." To cap things off, Gene joined Doris for her Columbia recording "Tea for Two." He taps alongside Day's vocal "Crazy Rhythm," then sings *and* taps for "I Know That You Know" and "Oh Me, Oh My, Oh You!" The album became a "Top 5" hit.

In 2019, Jeanine Basinger, cinema archivist at Wesleyan University, commented that Gene was a "lucky choice" for Doris' first screen dance partner. Basinger noted, "Nelson was a good-looking young man with an easy, athletic style of dance, a sort of relaxed Gene Kelly. He represents a male example of how musical stardom could elude a truly attractive and talented player. Nelson was an excellent dancer … and he was at ease in front of the camera."[117]  For his work in *Tea for Two*, Gene Nelson received 1950's Golden Globe Award for "New Star of the Year." The awards were held at Hollywood's Ciro's nightclub, on February 28, 1951. Gene was photographed shaking hands that evening with his idol Fred Astaire, who received a Golden Globe for his performance in the musical *Three Little Words.* Understandably, Gene felt that he had finally "arrived."

Next up, James Cagney. "Cagney was the first actor that ever hit me," Gene recalled in 1990, "and he taught me how to take a blow!"[118] "What a thrill that was," he enthused, while offering details about filming *The West Point Story.* In the summer of 1950, the two became good friends. After a day's shoot, Cagney would invite Gene to his dressing room. "He'd get the gin and tonic out," said Gene, "and by ten o'clock he'd be telling me about [his] days at Warner Brothers. Ah, he was such a marvelous man." There were lots of stories to tell, and Gene relished every moment. Cagney, who considered himself more of a "hoofer" than a tough guy, was making a return to musicals following his Oscar-winning role in *Yankee Doodle Dandy* (1942). *The West Point Story* was directed by Roy del Ruth, who had directed Cagney in three pre-Code Warner Bros. hits.

On screen, Cagney's punch into Gene's jaw was intended for an ornery producer (Roland Winters). Cagney lifts his knocked-out pal Gene into his arms and carries him off screen. While *The West Point Story* gave an obligatory nod to the military, it leaned towards gags, in what critic Leonard Maltin deemed a, "Silly, but watchable musical."[119] The plot stumbles along as has-been Broadway director Cagney, amid a flurry of temper-tantrums, pulls together West Point's annual revue written by cadets Tom (Gordon MacRae) and Hal (Gene Nelson). Cadets in drag were part of the deal. "All of our girls are men," MacRae informs Cagney, who immediately recruits his protegee Jan (Doris Day) from Hollywood. Also on hand is Cagney's gal Eve (Virginia Mayo), who pulls no punches, while keeping Cagney in queue.

***The West Point Story*** (1950) Nelson, Day, Cagney, Mayo, MacRae (WB)

Gene's dance numbers were slick, especially his two-minute tap sequence using a cane prop to the tune *Long Before I Knew You*. Fifth-billed, he also got to dance with Mayo for the *Military Polka*. Day, despite her delightful duets with MacRae, referred *The West Point Story* as "a real idiot picture."[120] Cagney's opinion? "Cornball as hell, but don't let anyone tell me that those songs … aren't worth listening to."[121] The film was nominated for an Academy Award for Best Music (Scoring of a Musical Picture). Over the next three years, Gene was pleased as *punch* whenever Cagney showed up to watch him dance on Warner Bros. soundstages.

<<>>

In May 1950, the studio announced that Gene would be reunited with June Haver in *Just off Broadway.* By the time rehearsals for the film began (August 21) the film was re-titled *Lullaby of Broadway,* and Gene's co-star was not Haver, but Doris Day. Haver had become disenchanted with Hollywood. On a personal note, a brief first marriage ended in divorce, and her next fiancé died under tragic circumstances. A devout Catholic, Haver considered becoming a nun. While shooting her final film for Fox, she suffered a concussion, which made her more determined to find religious refuge. "What I want must be what God wants," she told the media.[122] In February 1953, Haver became a postulant nun in Leavenworth, Kansas.[123] By the Spring of 1954, she was back in Hollywood and in the arms of Fred MacMurray. Their marriage was a happy and lasting one.

When I met June Haver (c.1970) it was at a shopping mall in Sonoma County, California. She and MacMurray had a ranch in nearby Healdsburg, where they found peace and solitude from the film industry. I saw my mother talking to June and walked over to them. Mother asked, "Scott, do you know who this is?" Haver interjected, "Oh, *he* won't know who I am. He's too young!" I promptly responded, "You're June Haver." The look of surprise on her face was one to treasure. She beamed while we chatted. Of course, I was an old movie buff. To me, June Haver had a relaxed and contented presence. She had made a successful departure from the limelight she had grown tired of.

It would take another three years for Gene Nelson—tired of how Warner Bros. was handling his career—to make a transition into free-lancing. While making *Lullaby of Broadway*, however, he felt the studio was seeing him in a new light. After all, he was Doris Day's leading man. The New York premier of *Lullaby* ... was greeted warmly. Critic Liza Wilson enthused, "Gene's dance numbers are exciting and excellently done ... and the boy is quite an actor." *Variety* chimed in, "Topflight musical comedy with eye-and-ear entertainment certain to catch attention ... Nelson dances in top form and his song numbers are delivered with enthusiasm."[124] Gene was partially dubbed by big-band vocalist Hal Derwin.[125] Gene disliked Warners' utilizing a voice double for his songs. The film buzzed with memorable melodies, including the title tune from Warner Bros. *Golddiggers of 1935*. The "deft direction" (as *Variety* put it) was by David Butler, who had helmed several Shirley Temple films in the 30's. The premise of the story was similar to director Frank Capra's hit *Lady for a Day* (1933).

The plot involved Day leaving an amateur musical tour in England, and sailing to New York in hopes to reunite with her actress mother. A flirtatious encounter aboard ship (with Nelson) ensues. She hasn't a clue that *he* is a professional Broadway dancer. She also hasn't a clue that mom (the poignant Gladys George), after guzzling away her career, has hit the skids, and is performing in Greenwich Village. Ironically, Day is protected from the truth while staying with a Hungarian beer brewer (S. Z. Sakall). Sakall encourages Day to co-star with his leading man (Nelson) in a musical he is backing (with his wife's money). The two co-stars connect romantically. As expected, an affectionate mother-daughter reunion allows for up-tempo entertainment filled with nostalgic tunes from years gone by.

***Lullaby of Broadway* (1951) (WB)**

Gene was dead set on dancing to *Zing! Went the Strings of My Heart*, in which he leaps atop a piano, before flying over the Page Cavanaugh Trio. Stunning stuff. When a fan tells him he's the best dancer in the world, Gene gets the one-liner: "It's you and me against Fred Astaire!" A dash of far-fetched humor has Gene getting suspicious of the Day-Sakall relationship. His low-key approach comes across as natural, and as to be expected, the Day-Nelson combo prevails. The duo team for classics like "You're Getting to be a Habit with Me" and "Somebody Loves Me" (cleverly maneuvering through glass doors), before a dazzling finish to the title tune. Technicolor photography (Wilfrid M. Cline) was at its best.

Long after the film's release, Gene complimented Day. "She was, of course, a musician by nature," said Gene, "so there was no problem with her timing, and she picked up the steps quite quickly. It's hard work … that takes days of constant practice. But she did it—beautifully."[126] In her 1975 memoir, Day confirmed, "My most difficult dance routines were in *Lullaby of Broadway*." She arrived on the set for the film's finale, and was confronted with what she called "a Mount Everest of stairs." "You've got to be out of your minds!" she yelled. It was Miriam who induced Day to join Gene doing spins and turns up-and-down "Mount Everest." Dressed in a heavy, floor-length gold lamé ball-gown didn't help matters. "But somehow," Day acknowledged, "we got that dance in the can. I would have preferred to dive off the Golden Gate Bridge."[127]

**_Lullaby_ ... leading man for Doris Day (WB)**

**Chris and Gene on the set of _Lullaby of Broadway_**

<><>

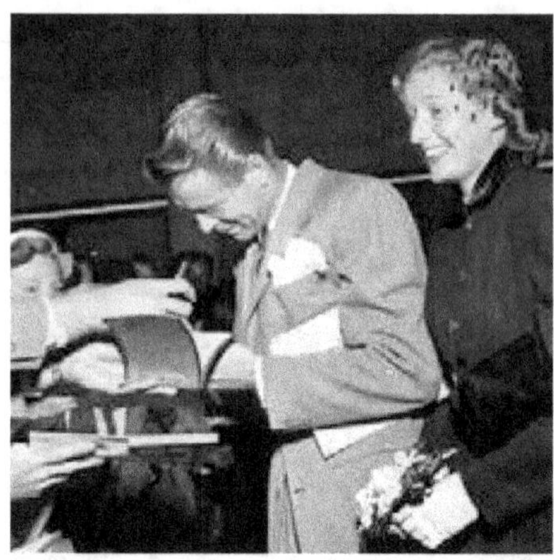

**Gene and Miriam meet the fans**

Shortly after the release of *Lullaby of Broadway* (April 1951), columnist Sidney Skolsky indicated that Gene Nelson "receives more fan mail than any other actor at his studio. This indicates that people want to see him in the movies."[128] While his popularity soared, Gene relished the time he was able to be at home and work on various projects. He put in a new lawn, knocked out walls, and painted the interior. If the plumbing broke down, he could fix it. He enjoyed cooking outdoors on his rotating barbeque. "Our friendship with Gordon and Sheila MacRae also grew during this time," recalled Miriam. "We had a lot in common."[129] While papa Gene barbequed, Chris enjoyed playing with the three MacRae kids: Meredith, Heather and Gar.

Gene and Miriam had a group of chums called "The Mouse Pack," which included Gordon and Sheila, Marge and Gower Champion, Tony Curtis and Janet Leigh, songwriter Sammy Cahn, and screenwriter and future director Blake Edwards. Miriam detailed, "The Mouse Pack got together on weekends to cook and swim. We frequently went to the Champion's house off Sunset. We always sat down in front of the television, eating off TV trays, so we could watch *Your Hit Parade.*" Some days the guys would wash their cars together, while the women cooked. Evenings at the MacRae's always ended with a game of charades. "The Mouse

Pack" was a take-off of "The Rat Pack" which originated with Humphrey Bogart and Lauren Bacall—later to be helmed by original pack member Frank Sinatra on the Las Vegas strip.[130] In 1999, Marge Champion confirmed, "We weren't eligible for The Rat Pack."[131] Bogart and clan considered themselves non-conformists. The sweetheart image that clung to Gene, Miriam and the others didn't make the grade, and they couldn't care less. Besides, as 1951 came to a close, Miriam, Gene and Chris were focused on a new addition to their family. Miriam was expecting!

**Mouse Pack chums: Miriam, Gene, Gordon, Sheila**

*Painting the Clouds with Sunshine* (1951) "Mambo Man" with Virginia Mayo (WB)

*Crime Wave* (1954) with Sterling Hayden (WB)

# More Musicals and - a Dash of Noir

Warner Bros. reached into the vault for Gene's next film. The story was a loose adaptation of the pre-Code gem *Gold Diggers of 1933*, along with its memorable hit tune "We're in the Money." The studio didn't exactly rake in the dough with *Painting the Clouds with Sunshine*, but *Variety* admitted, "its entertainment values cannot be ignored." For this version, gold-digger Virginia Mayo (in a role turned down by Doris Day) went to Las Vegas to snag a millionaire. The studio was, in fact, vacillating about calling it *Gold Diggers of Las Vegas.* Gene provides charisma as Ted Lansing, a millionaire in disguise. Reviews found his dancing to be a major asset, rescuing viewers from a patchwork plot. It all takes place at The Golden Egg casino owned by the befuddled S.Z. Sakall. "Mambo Man" had Gene playing bongos at The Golden Egg, while doing a rhumba with Mayo. More steam was generated by the duo in "Birth of the Blues"—as Gene's lips pucker up to a trumpet for the *entire* routine—an impressive feat. Offscreen, jazzman Ziggy Elman did the actual trumpeting.

Dennis Morgan, first-billed as an impulsive gambler, pairs off with mezzo-soprano Lucille Norman, and Gene is drawn to the likeable Virginia Gibson, who had danced in *Tea for Two*. Mayo's millionaire is Gene's priggish cousin (Tom Conway). The film closed with a Vegas hoedown, in which Gene and Gibson do a clever dance routine ("Arkansas Traveler") with a jackass. Gene finally grabs a lasso for some fancy spinning—a sneak preview of his impressive turn in *Oklahoma!* David Butler, directing Gene for the fourth and last time, commented on *Painting the Clouds with Sunshine* in 1977, saying: "I think that was the worst of the whole bunch I made—I thought it was terrible."[132]

In the summer of 1951, Gene was recruited to entertain servicemen at Travis Air Force Base (near San Francisco). G.I.'s at Travis were headed for combat in Korea. Wounded servicemen were recovering at the base. Echoing Warner Bros. *This is the Army* and *Hollywood Canteen*, the all-star tribute *Starlift* (1951) included Gene, Doris Day, Gordon MacRae, Virginia Mayo and Ruth Roman. Cameos included Cagney and Gary Cooper. The point: to boost patriotism. Gene's first number takes place in Hollywood. He joins Janice Rule for a flamenco-style dance to Cole Porter's "What Is This Thing Called Love?" Nicely done. At Travis, Gene shows up in uniform, teaming with Janice for some humorous up-tempo tapping to the Doris Day hit, "It's Magic."

### *Starlift* (1951) WB

*Starlift* was basically "a flimsy account" (as Leonard Maltin puts it) of a G.I. (Ron Hagerthy) attempting to woo an actress (Janice

Rule). His scheme works, but the result is less than convincing. Doris Day's medley of tunes holds interest during the first segment of *Starlift*. She's a joy to listen to. Subsequent routines seem forced, especially an overlong segment with card shark wannabe Phil Harris. In his *Korean War Filmography* (2003) author Robert J. Lentz noted, "The Korean experience changed the way Americans viewed war. The lack of a clear-cut victory inspired filmmakers to try to make sense of fighting another country's civil war and risking American lives for an unpopular cause."[133] 54,000 American troops (and 18 women on active duty) lost their lives. As for *Starlift*, Lentz summed up, "The film is far less effective than it should have been, and not particularly patriotic." The word "Korea" isn't uttered on screen. There actually was an "Operation Starlift" (spearheaded by Ruth Roman), but major studios neglected to carry the operating costs. The project folded prior to the film's release.[134] *The New York Times* indicated that it had become "a slightly embarrassing subject in Hollywood."

As *Starlift* hit screens for the Christmas holidays, the Nelsons were anticipating a new little brother or sister for Christopher. It would be a dream come true. Gene had acknowledged, "Miriam and I would like to have more children and a larger permanent home to raise them in. If things keep going as well as they have been these last two years, we may get them both by our eleventh anniversary. It's certainly worth dreaming and working for."[135] Gene told the press that Chris was "no help at all" when it came to choosing a name for the baby. When asked for some suggestions, the youngster responded, "Christopher like me, if it's a boy. Poofentoot, like our cat, if it's a girl."[136] Miriam and Gene were both hoping for a girl. Sadly, *Variety* reported that Miriam lost her "prematurely born baby."[137] The infant daughter was born on January 1, 1952, in Los Angeles. Records indicate that her burial at the Chapel of the Pines Crematory took place on January 3rd.[138] The Nelsons made no comment to the press. Miriam would have no more children.

Gene and Miriam had several weeks to console each other before Warner's assigned Gene to a 10-week tour on the East Coast. At the end of February, his twenty-minute act began in Chicago. Wearing a tux and top-hat, he came on stage to the strains of "Lullaby of Broadway," leaping atop an upright piano. *Variety* commented on the "moans and groans" from female members in the audience as he danced with an imaginary partner to the dreamy strains of "Laura." Gene closed with vigorous ballet moves for "St. Louis Blues." *Variety* nodded: "Blonde terper has charm and does a terrific selling job, backed by a boundless enthusiasm."[139] As the tour wound up at New York's Warner Theatre, *Variety* added, "the smooth and ingratiating terper shows much charm and skill and has some applause-winning routines. However … he talks too much."[140] The Newspaper Guild didn't mind Nelson's gab. They invited him to the Page One Ball at the Hotel Astor. Gene had the honor of accepting the "Page One Award" on behalf of Vivien Leigh, for her Academy Award-winning performance in *A Streetcar Named Desire*.[141]

**March 17, 1952 – Miriam & Gene – "Out of This World Series"**

Between gigs, Gene flew home to connect with Miriam and Chris. In March, he was recruited for the Hollywood Entertainers

Baseball Game at Gilmore Field. The annual "Out of This World Series" included team players Elizabeth Taylor, Mickey Rooney, and Marilyn Monroe, who swung the bat in high heels! Not to be outdone by Monroe, Gene found himself doing high-kicks in front of an atomic bomb! While performing in Las Vegas, he was sought out by photographer Don English. In 2000, English recalled Gene's publicity stunt during the atomic testing that was making headlines.

> *We took a guy named Gene Nelson, a dancer playing at the Desert Inn Hotel. His show went late, he probably got through around 2 a.m. At 3:30 or 4:00 in the morning we went to the mountain [Frenchman's Flat] to shoot a blast of the atom bomb. ... He did some dancing ... with the atom bomb in the background. We didn't have a feeling of the ramifications. We were innocent in that we didn't know the danger of radiation.*[142]

Forty miles away from the blast, Gene couldn't resist doing what he called the "Atom Antic" –leaping into the air with arms and legs reaching into infinity. As photographer English pointed out, the dangers of nuclear fallout were relatively unknown. The health consequences (cancer) of radioactive poison would haunt generations to come who lived in the surrounding area. The federal government (contrary to what science indicated) assured residents that atomic tests posed no serious threat.

**April 1952 - "Atomic Antic" - Las Vegas**

Warner Bros. sent Gene on another junket to promote *She's Working Her Way Through College*. Miriam tagged along, as did newlyweds Ronald and Nancy Reagan. "We traveled across country by train," recalled Miriam in 2009. "Warners' representatives would meet us at the station … to the pop and flash of the local *paparazzi*. We were driven to the best hotel in town as if we were royalty. We'd usually meet with town dignitaries. Then we'd visit the local Veterans' or children's hospital where we'd circulate from one bed to another. Faces like the veterans and the especially the children have stuck with me all these years."[143]

In Springfield, Missouri, they dined with President Truman. Afterward, they rode in open cars down main street following Truman, who walked the entire route! "He was a feisty little man," noted Miriam. Reagan emceed their stints with Nancy at his side. In their skit, Nancy would freeze up. Reagan whispered into her ear what to say. Inevitably, she would mention her "handsome, wonderful husband." The Reagans left the tour early. Gene and Miriam became emcees for the remaining gigs, using the same skit. While in Memphis, one future musical icon made a concerted effort to see them, albeit from a distance: Elvis Presley.

*She's Working Her Way Through College* costarred Gene, Reagan and Virginia Mayo. DC's *Evening Star* was incredulous that Warner Bros. had produced "a woefully diluted version" of the wise and witty play, *The Male Animal* (1940). The play was a proponent of free-speech. In 2020, TCM host Ben Mankiewicz pointed out Warner Bros.' inability to tackle the original plot, due to Hollywood being in the grip of anti-communist attitudes that "had seized control of the industry." The original political theme was discarded. Mayo played "Hot-Garters Gertie," a burlesque queen who desires a college degree to become a playwright. She succeeds. Encouraged by theater arts professor Reagan, she turns her play "The Gay and the Bold" ("Not a bad title," Reagan tells her) into a musical. After her controversial past is exposed, the liberal-leaning Reagan, following a cringe-worthy drunk scene, comes to her defense. His words to the student body are pertinent and have bite. The show goes on. As the school's star quarterback, Nelson is enamored with Gertie and joins the cast. *The New York Times* declared, "Mr. Nelson is especially exciting in one solo number he does—a combination of dancing and gymnastics that is the best single thing in the show."[144] In a cast of frantic cardboard characters, Nelson comes across as genuine, although his romance with Mayo feels a tad tentative at the finish. Released soon after MGM's classic *Singin' in the Rain* (1952), the glamour and clamor of *She's Working* ... paled in comparison. Even so, the film did well at the box-office. In her 2001 memoirs, Mayo, whose limber moves were nicely on display in the film, reflected,

> *She's Working Her Way Through College remains my all-time favorite movie. There is a dance scene where Gene Nelson dances (and does acrobatics) alone in a gymnasium, and it is a classic. I can't think of any other dance scene anywhere that can match this—it is amazing and compelling to watch. The man swings from the rings, throws himself over the horses and the parallel bars, flies across the mats, and even sings while hanging from a rope. What an athlete Gene Nelson was. ... And oh, what a sweet man. ... Guess it's fairly obvious that I loved Gene and we had a great time together. I was honored to work with him. He was one of those rare ones who also insisted in rehearsing and rehearsing. And rehearsing! Gene didn't tolerate mistakes. Nor did I.*[145]

**She's Working Her Way Through College** (1952) with **Mayo and Reagan (WB)**

Gene agreed to film the gymnasium scene *after* the film was completed. Producer William Jacobs didn't fancy the risk of Nelson injuring himself and holding up production. This allowed him to prep and rehearse for three months. The shoot itself took four days.[146] A review from *Seattle Daily Times* concurred with Mayo, saying, "It is Nelson who steals the show with a brilliant dance number that places him in a class with Gene Kelly and Fred Astaire."[147]

Gene would cross paths with future President Reagan years later, while dating Reagan's daughter Maureen. It was obvious that Reagan had changed his mind about "The Gay and the Bold." Gene attempted to reassure an upset Ronnie and Nancy that just because their son Ron Jr. enjoyed ballet, didn't necessarily mean that he was gay. More on that strange interlude, later.

In a radio interview with ex-heavyweight champ Max Baer, Gene indicated, "I would like to split up my pictures. Rather than do four musicals a year, I hope, when I'm a little more established, they let me do two musical pictures and maybe a couple of dramatic pictures. I'm dying to make a Western. I want to get on that horse. I love to ride."[148] Gene almost got his wish in 1957. Before the cameras rolled, he got "on that horse" alright. The horse reared up and …. (well, let's not get ahead of ourselves).

August 1952. Gene began filming another Technicolor flick with Virginia Mayo, *She's Back on Broadway.* Author James Robert Parish points out in *The Forties Gals*, the word "She's" was a ploy to "induce Virginia's fans into believing it was a sequel to *She's Working Her Way Through College.*"[149] It wasn't. Gene got second-billing in what was essentially a supporting role. His character tagged along for the ride. Fourth-billed Steve Cochran, a Broadway producer, was the guy who got Mayo, a Hollywood star trying to jump-start her sagging career. Cochran's sulky edge dominates the film. Musical numbers feel disconnected. Gene shines in a Mardi Gras number, wherein he spins, taps, and slides amidst a flurry of balloons. Otherwise, he shows up as a dance prop for Mayo. *Film Bulletin* summed up, "This Warner film musical-drama tries hard to be something worthwhile, but doesn't succeed. It just doesn't jell." Gene objected to being cast in the film. Years later, he observed, "They really didn't have a part for me, so they just invented one in order to fit me in to do the dances. I thought I deserved a little better."[150] *Motion Picture Daily* confirmed, "Nelson turns in two splendid dance numbers, but has nothing to do with the story proper."[151] Before her contract ended, WB decided to "hold the Mayo" when it came to musicals. *She's Back on Broadway* would be her last.

***She's Back on Broadway*** **(1953) with Virginia Mayo (WB)**

Gene lost his childhood mentor and inspiration just before filming *She's Back on Broadway*. His father, Leander Berg, passed away on August 7, 1952, at the age of sixty-seven. The 1952 Register of Voters indicated that he and Lenore (both Democrats) still resided on Pine Street in Santa Monica. An Associated Press report indicated that Lee Berg (as friends and co-workers referred to him) succumbed to "a lingering illness" and was still employed at Douglas Aircraft.[152]

In late November 1952, Gene reported to the Los Angeles Police Department Homicide Division. The reason? He was selected by Warner Bros. to replace Steve Cochran in the moody, menacing noir *Crime Wave*.[153] Jack Warner wanted Humphrey Bogart and Ava Gardner for the leads, but when director Andre DeToth protested, Warner cut his budget. A camera catering to big name stars would compromise the effect DeToth was after. He confirmed later on, "When I went to Jack's office to talk about *Crime Wave*, he screamed, 'What the hell are you thinking of? I offer you Bogart and Ava Gardner. You don't want them?'" DeToth said no. "Go ahead," said Jack, "make the goddamned picture with nobodies. Cut your own throat. You'll have to shoot it in fifteen days. Go on, get out."[154]

As a newlywed ex-con, Nelson tackled the role of Steve Lacy, who is caught between the machinations of ex-San Quentin cellmates and an unrelenting homicide detective (Sterling Hayden). Lacy, an airplane mechanic (ironic employment for Leander Berg's son), is trying to go straight. He is suddenly forced to cooperate in a bank robbery, or else! His wife (Phyllis Kirk) is held hostage. Lacy doesn't exactly trust the law, but reluctantly agrees to be, as he puts it, Hayden's "pet rat." Nelson brought a sense of foreboding to the noir equation, which was both vulnerable and natural. In 2013, writer Laura Wagner made note of Nelson's dramatic turn, saying, "Gene Nelson is excellent as the handsome young mechanic trying to have a better life. He and Phyllis Kirk have an appealing chemistry, and there's a nice steamy undercurrent to their relationship. I'd have liked to see Nelson do more roles of this type. He was certainly a multitalented man."[155] In 1954, a critic for *Philadelphia Inquirer* acknowledged, "Apparently, an excellent actor has been buried all these years under the musical froth, for Nelson's Steve Lacy is his best screen job to date."[156]

***Crime Wave* (1954) with Phyllis Kirk (WB)**

Besides Sterling Hayden's toughness, Charles Bronson (billed as Charles Buchinsky) shows up as one of the escapees who insist that Lacy help with the bank heist. Bronson's menace is chilling.

*Time* magazine referred to the film as a "Muscular little thriller that carries more conviction than many more high-toned movie melodramas." Cinematographer Bert Glennon melds into DeToth's vision of a smoggy, gritty Los Angeles. Although completed in December 1952, *Crime Wave* wasn't released until March 1954. Most likely, Warner was still upset about "the goddamned picture with nobodies." There was a preview at the Los Angeles Pantages in 1953, which Nelson attended. One columnist noted the audience's applause for "Gene's first dramatic triumph."[157] The film was using the title *The City is Dark* at that juncture. *Photoplay* contributing editor Janet Graves thought *The City is Dark* "topnotch." "Matter-of-fact, unpretentious, played throughout in low key," stated Graves, "this expertly written, shrewdly filmed crime drama is quite a hunk of movie. Gene Nelson, without singing one note or dancing one tap, plays a troubled parolee with sympathy and conviction."[158]

Hungarian-American director DeToth helmed *Crime Wave* just prior to making the popular 3-D thriller *House of Wax*. Gene himself would venture into the world of sci-fi in *The Atomic Man* (1955). While Gene was discouraged with how Warner Bros. was handling his career, he had *no* idea how life-changing his next and final film for the studio would be.

*Three Sailors and a Girl* (1953) with Jane Powell (WB)

# Chapter 7

# Scandal ... into Freelancing

As mentioned, Miriam was fully aware of the "pressure" women placed on Gene to stray. His 1948 affair with Dorothy Babb seemed to have quashed his vulnerability. In her memoirs, Miriam indicated there were no further problems over the next four years. Then, during February 1953, filming began for Gene's final Warner Bros. film, *Three Sailors and a Girl*. MGM soprano Jane Powell was borrowed for the female lead. It's was Powell's first loan-out since signing with Metro in 1943. She was eager to branch out from playing the protected innocents she portrayed in MGM musicals. She got her wish ... offscreen.

Powell's talent and screen presence were undeniable. For *Three Sailors and a Girl* Gordon MacRae was assigned the male lead, with Gene in queue to dance with Jane. After a film preview, *Harrison Reports* indicated that Powell "more than holds her own in several nimble-footed dance routines with Gene Nelson."[159] The choreography was first-rate. Nelson's inventive and risky dance at an auto garage was in full gear. The vocal blend of Powell and MacRae was another plus. Jane's clever rendition of "Kiss Me or I'll Scream!" was a delight. Even so, *Harrison Reports* concluded, "On the whole ... it is an unimaginative picture and its running time is much too long for what it has to offer."

Based on a 1925 George S. Kaufman play (*The Butter and Egg Man*), *Three Sailors and Girl* involved three gobs, on leave in New York, who invest a great deal of cash (mostly from fellow crew members) in a Broadway musical. In-your-face producer Sam Levene manipulates them with lies and fast-talk. Somehow, a potential flop is diverted into a hit by Powell and her three sailor chums. Comedian Jack E. Leonard played the third gob. *Variety* noted the "spritely performances" coupled with "plot hokum" as being "expertly blended" by director Roy Del Ruth. It was a generous assessment. *The New York Times* summed up: "This misguided attempt at light entertainment thuds along close to rock bottom."[160] Despite the best efforts of the star-trio, a cliché-ridden scenario lets them down—all the more reason for Gene Nelson to leave Warner Bros. In a 1982 interview, Nelson mentioned MGM as being a "progressive, creative atmosphere." "Warner was too cheap," he emphasized, adding that Jack Warner was capitalizing on the studio that was leading the way.[161] As fate would have it, according to Jane Powell, "MGM wouldn't allow Gene to set foot on the lot once we started going together."[162]

Gene and Jane connected in ways that jolted the Hollywood community. While extra-marital affairs among stars were commonplace, Powell's youthful, wholesome screen image belied her ability for such "misconduct." She and Gene became fodder for fan magazine gossip and scandal. In her 1988 autobiography *The Girl Next Door ... and How She Grew*, Powell reflected on her connection to Gene. "He was sweet, and at first it was just nice to have someone to talk to. That's what started it all—talking. Then one thing led to another. I fell head over heels in love."[163] Powell's own backstory explains a great deal.

**1953 - Jane and Gene at Ciro's**

At the age of fourteen, Jane signed with MGM. Childhood had centered on *her* becoming the next Shirley Temple, *her* becoming the bread-winner for the family. As Powell put it, "I fulfilled my parents dreams."[164] Her parents' troubled marriage, amplified by separations and alcohol abuse, would end in divorce. Jane's 1949 marriage to Geary Steffen, an insurance broker, allowed her to escape unhappy circumstances, but not for long. Powell indicated that despite having a small son and infant daughter, she was troubled with her own marriage. Eager to tie the marital knot with Gene, she filed for divorce from Steffen in August 1953.[165]

Miriam's petition for divorce stated that she and Gene separated on April 10, 1953, just as filming completed on *Three Sailors and a Girl*. Miriam detailed, "they say the wife is always the last to know. In this case, I was the *first*. I grew suspicious about the time Jane brought a cake to the house. I asked Gene if he was having an affair and he admitted he was. It's probably not an understatement to say I was devastated. I told him to get out!"[166] Gene and Powell talked about marriage, but Gene eventually backed off. As Powell later recalled, Gene "went off to think things over."

Complicating Gene's plans to move forward involved money matters. Miriam's divorce petition made it difficult for him to contemplate supporting two households. With his Warner income gone, he found himself on tour, freelancing. Locations for his nightclub act included Toronto, Miami, The Cocoanut Grove, and the Sahara in Las Vegas. For the Vegas stint he was co-billed with opera diva Marguerite Piazza, after she refused to be billed below transgender pioneer Christine Jorgensen.[167] Television also beckoned. Gene Nelson's visibility was kept steady with a string of guest appearances on popular shows for the small screen.

**July 1953 – Las Vegas – Gene replaced transgender pioneer Christine Jorgensen**

When Gene had custody of his son Chris, the two spent time at horse shows and going fishing. Despite his busy schedule, Gene found time to explore another passion: flying lessons near Palm Springs. There was talk of him wanting to return to Miriam, but she was unwilling. "There would be months of intense emotion," said Miriam. "Anger, resentment, fear, grief and depression. It was not easy for me, someone who liked being in control of her emotions."[168] She emphasized in her memoir, "All of our mutual friends—every single one—continued to be friends with *me*. That's not to say they didn't have contact with Gene or that they didn't sympathize with him … Everyone from The Mouse Pack kept calling and insisting I come back to the Sunday parties. Of course, Gene was no longer a part of the group."[169] Years later, Jane Powell reflected on how she and Gene were treated, saying, "We were ostracized, like we had leprosy."[170] As fate would have it, all the Mouse Pack members who came to Miriam's defense would eventually, over the ensuing years, divorce their own spouses.

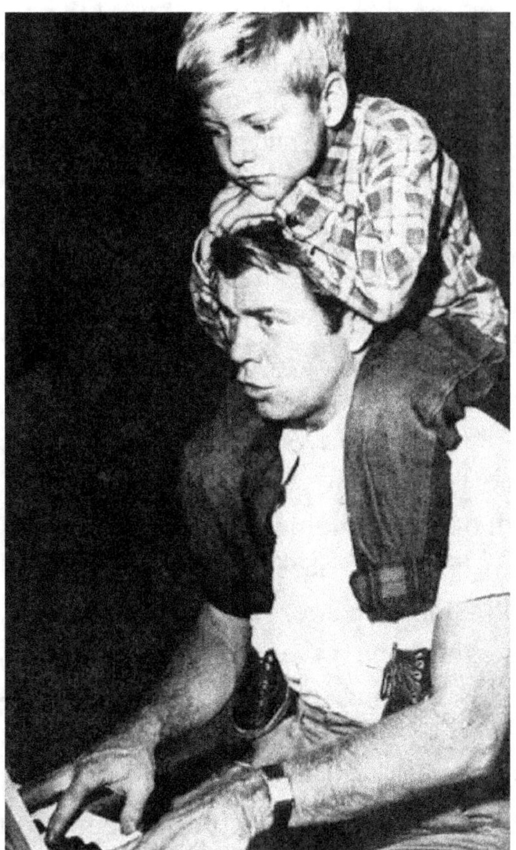

**Early 1954 – Gene and Chris**

Following her divorce, Powell was desperate. She hated being alone. A blind date with auto dealer Pat Nerney (former husband of actress Mona Freeman) would lead to marriage the following year (1954). Nerney would be the second of Jane Powell's five marriages. She was frank regarding her insecurities, saying: "Because I was so inexperienced and knew so little about men, each time I was attracted to someone, or he was attracted to me, I fell in love. And each time, I felt I should get married—and usually did."[171] It could be that Gene sensed this about Jane and resolved to have a time-out. His and Miriam's own divorce wouldn't become final until June 1956.

In the Spring of 1968, I had the good fortune to meet Jane Powell backstage in San Francisco. She had been a particular favorite of mine since childhood. During her performance at the nightclub Bimbo's 365, she included hits from her MGM films, and a heartfelt rendition of the current Jimmie Rodgers Grammy-nominated "Child of Clay"–which focused on the challenges facing the younger generation. Powell was smiling and gracious during our conversation. She cared. Looking back, although I was unfamiliar with her affair with Gene Nelson, I was impressed with her sensitivity and engaging personality. In 1987, Jane indicated that she and Gene were still in touch: "I still talk to him, every so often, and we exchange cards for birthdays and at Christmas."[172]

In the aftermath of all the drama, Jane Powell had the good fortune to star in one of her most successful films *Seven Brides for Seven Brothers* (1954) – nominated for Best Picture. Miriam, with the help of her almost-ex-husband's credit card, got a new wardrobe and lightened her hair, creating a new image as she re-established her career as choreographer. "Gene almost had a stroke when he got the bill!" she admitted. Gene's screen career was in limbo. His contract with Warner Bros. was not renewed. It would be almost a year before he made another film. In the fall of 1953, it was reported that he was being paged to play jazz-showman Ted Lewis in a Broadway musical, "Hat, Cane and Hands"—a project that never reached fruition. It was also announced that Gene would be Sonja Henie's leading man when she made her film comeback in Cinemascope and "lavish, Technicolor."[173] Instead of Sonja, Gene would finally hook up on screen with former Mouse Pack pal Tony Curtis.

<<>>

**The Bob Hope Show – December 18, 1953 (NBC)**

Gene became a familiar face on TV screens after leaving Warner Bros. By 1954, sixty percent of American homes had televisions—up to 26 million viewers. While movie attendance began to drop off, Gene danced for *Your Show of Shows*—a "live" variety show. On Ed Sullivan's *Toast of the Town* Gene danced to the "St. Louis Blues." Following his stunning (and hilarious) turn as a dancer who goes for psychiatric counseling on the *Colgate Comedy Hour* (November 1953), Gene was invited back (January 1954) to banter with Ethel Merman and Jimmy Durante. His solo dance whirl had him crashing into things and destroying props, before offering a spot-on impersonation of Durante, saying, "You know … some days it just don't pay to get up!" On *The Bob Hope Show*, Gene (paired with dancer Pat Horn) offered a six-minute contemporary dance version of Tchaikovsky's "Nutcracker Suite"—he was "the sandman" in a young boy's dream—offering a dazzling display of spins and twirls, ballet and jazz. Afterward, Bob joined Gene for a soft-shoe routine to the vintage tune "Narcissus."

In late March 1954, Gene reported to Universal-International to film the musical-comedy *So This is Paris.* On screen, audiences followed three U.S. sailors, at liberty, in France. A wild venture through the French countryside, had the trio dance atop a taxi, frolic with damsels on a haystack, and hitch a ride on the *outside* of a bus (as only Gene Nelson could have envisioned)—a fun, fantasy-laden venture. Gene's choreography literally carries the film forward on this and several other occasions. Otherwise, the scenario tends to lose steam. Once in gay Paree, the focus is on frantic, stereotypical flirtations. The grand finale had our three gobs promoting a far-fetched benefit show for French war orphans. *Film Bulletin* summed up *So This is Paris* as a "slick, featherweight musical … for escapist audiences." *Dance Magazine* saw the light as far as any "freshness" the film offered, saying, "Most of the credit clearly belongs to Nelson himself." Following previews, it was announced that Tony, Gene and third gob Paul Gilbert would reteam for *So This is Rio.* When that didn't happen, no one seemed to mind.

As co-star *and* choreographer, Gene had the opportunity to coach Tony Curtis in his first (and only) musical. Tony had to admit, "Whoever said dancing was sissy stuff ought to try a few routines with Gene."[174] Curtis was fortunate to be coached by Gene Nelson, as opposed to Gene Kelly. Kelly was a "tough" taskmaster on co-stars who danced with him.[175] In 2008, Curtis recalled:

> *Nelson, who staged all the dance numbers, helped me learn the steps. He said, "Put your hand on my shoulder. When you feel my weight shift, you shift. He was really the first person who really taught me how to dance.*[176]

***So This is Paris* (1954) rehearsing with Tony Curtis (UI)**

Upon the film's release, *Film Bulletin* barbed, "Tony Curtis fans should be happily surprised by their idol's handling of his hoof-and-mouth assignments."[177] A critic for the *New York Post*, wasn't surprised at all, countering, "Tony Curtis. There's nothing wrong with him that staying out of musicals won't cure. This simply isn't his dish of smorgasbord."[178] When Los Angeles reporter Howard McClay visited the set of *So This is Paris,* he observed Gene gracefully sail above a Volkswagen, vault over a bicyclist, scale up a building in pursuit of a flirtatious mademoiselle, and finally leap off a balcony to land on a passerby's shoulders. As the lyrics indicated, he was "Lookin' for Someone to Love." McClay was awestruck. "I can't blame anyone but *myself* for that routine," said Gene with a breathless grin. McClay indicated that he hadn't seen such footwork since watching old Douglas Fairbanks Sr. films. Gene nodded, "You may be kidding, but you've hit the nail on the head. I've always been an admirer of Fairbanks. Some dancers work a lifetime to acquire the agility and natural grace that was his. And when I think of a number like the one I just completed, I think of it in terms of how Fairbanks might have done it."[179] And like Fairbanks, an occasional injury interfered.

During the last week of filming, Gene made a bad landing and twisted his back. Suffering from a herniated disc, he was able to finish by taking pain pills. As he explained it, "I went to a surgeon who advised an operation, but I wanted to avoid that." Another doctor suggested therapy. "The first part of that," said Gene, "was to get me off codeine, on which I was becoming hooked. I switched to about twelve Bufferins a day, being taped up, and a lot of rest."[180] For all the life's blood (and pain) Gene Nelson put into *So This is Paris*, he received third billing, below that of Gloria DeHaven, who was Curtis' love interest (on and off screen). Upon release, The National Legion of Decency deemed it necessary to give *So This is Paris* a "B" rating for "suggestive dancing."[181] Could it have been the musical strip-tease offered by Gene, Tony and Paul Gilbert? Yep, right down to their undies, while they admired each other's shortcomings.

***So This is Paris*** (1954) Beefcake on screen (UI)

**So This is Paris** (1954) Tony, Gene, and Gloria DeHaven (UI)

While Mouse Pack members Tony Curtis and Janet Leigh were busy consoling Miriam Nelson, Curtis, as mentioned, was having his own romantic affair with co-star Gloria DeHaven. In his 2008 memoirs, Curtis was frank about his feelings. "Gloria was a beautiful, gracious woman, and I wanted her badly. When we were doing the picture, she let me know it was okay for me to come after her, so between shots we started a relationship. ... She never once put any pressure on me to get a divorce and marry her."[182] At the time, DeHaven was in the process of divorcing her husband of less than a year. Tony and Gloria continued to see each other until, according to Curtis, "everyday life intervened." Publicity hounds failed to sniff out this romantic interlude. Mr. and Mrs. Curtis, three years into marriage, escaped the kind of scandal that engulfed Gene and Miriam Nelson.

"Everyday life" intervened in a good way for Gene Nelson at this juncture. In June 1954, it was announced that he had been assigned the coveted role of Will Parker in a film version of Broadway's hit *Oklahoma!* In July, Gene and other cast members headed for on-location shooting, *not* in Oklahoma, but Arizona!

*Oklahoma!* (1955) as Will Parker performing "Kansas City" (RKO)

# Chapter 8

# *Oklahoma!*

In August 1954, Gene hightailed it from Arizona and flew to New York for a sneak preview of *So This is Paris.* "He liked what he saw," said columnist Sheilah Graham, "then headed back to … his role in *Oklahoma!* He'll soon have enough money in the bank to make a settlement with estranged wife Miriam."[183] Miriam herself had contracted to do choreography for popular TV shows as *Colgate Comedy Hour*, *Shower of Stars*, and "The Judy Garland Special" (*Ford Star Jubilee*). In 1955, she would help create the most significant film of her career: *Picnic* (nominated for Best Picture). Miriam (uncredited) staged the unforgettable cinematic moment when William Holden and Kim Novak slow-danced to the sensual, haunting beat of "Moonglow" entwined with the film's theme song. While Gene and Miriam's reconciliation attempts had failed, their careers were very much intact.

Gene was on the mend from his herniated disc when he auditioned for *Oklahoma!* Agnes de Mille, who had choreographed the original Broadway production, specifically chose Gene for the part of Will Parker. "I was in agony," recalled Gene, "but I didn't tell her or anybody else. I did an audition for her and got the part, and I went through all the rehearsals taped up. Every moment I wasn't working I was in my dressing room, either sitting or lying down. I finally took the tape off the day we started to shoot "Kansas City" on location in Arizona."[184]

Richard Rodgers and Oscar Hammerstein, who collaborated on *Oklahoma!* (1943)—made sure the Broadway run and national tour were complete before Hollywood got its hungry hands on it. Director Fred Zinnemann, who received an Academy Award for *From Here to Eternity* (1953), was chosen for his ability as a "realist" who would avoid the "gloss" that film musicals leaned upon. Arizona, compensated for the lack of suitable rural areas in Oklahoma. Even so, crews had to plant ten acres of wheat and corn. The musical was an adaptation of the play *Green Grow the Lilacs* (1931), about settlers in Oklahoma's Cherokee Nation. "The governor of Oklahoma was irate that they were going to shoot *Oklahoma!* in Arizona," recalled Gene. After all, in 1953, "Oklahoma!" became the state's official song. Governor Johnston Murray made, what Nelson designated as, a "politically wise move" by visiting the film location. Murray (jokingly) declared the area as a territory of Oklahoma. "I thought it was kinda cute," mused Gene, "and very successful publicity-wise!"[185]

Director and "realist" Zinnemann went so far as to send someone to Oklahoma to record people's accents. In 1983, Gene detailed, "They found one man who was not an actor, just to read one page of my part. They did that for all the characters. Then they made a record … and gave one to each of us. It was to capture that real Oklahoma accent … not southern, but that wonderful, good Oklahoma sound." Gene chuckled, "Hell, I spoke with that accent for two months after we finished the picture. I just couldn't stop."[186]

*Oklahoma!* had the turn-of-the-century "look" and "feel" in which the story was set. For the "Kansas City" number, cast and crew headed to the Old West atmosphere of Eglin, Arizona, with its rustic, retro train depot. The scene was a standout for many reasons. Together, Agnes De Mille and Gene Nelson recreated the scenario. "Agnes invented a lot of the choreography on the spot," recalled Gene. "She didn't know much about tap dancing and we would discuss bits of business and she'd say, 'Show me some steps.' I would, and then she'd say, 'That's good, let's do that.' The basis of her choreography was character … She had analyzed Will Parker and figured out what the man would do to express himself. That was her technique. She built the number around me."[187]

After four weeks' rehearsal, the scene was shot. Gene began by squatting down to offer details about Kansas City, where, according to Will, "they've gone about as fer as they can go!" His mellow baritone describes what he saw in that sinful town. The other cowpokes hoot, holler and gather 'round to hear more. After a two-step with Aunt Eller (Charlotte Greenwood), he demonstrates a ragtime step, allowing a horse to lick his neck—all on cue. After twirling around a post, Gene goes into high gear until his boots crash through a wooden crate. Everyone chuckles and gets into the swing of two-stepping. Gene choreographs a moment where he kicks his hat off his own head! He then grabs a lariat, twirling it madly, jumping in and out of it. As a train leaves the station, he's doing high-kicks atop the caboose. It's easy to understand why De Mille told Gene, "That's good, let's do that.'"

Musical numbers for *Oklahoma!* were integrated into the narrative with finesse. Gordon MacRae and Shirley Jones, in her film debut, were *Oklahoma*'s engaging romantic leads. From MacRae's "Oh! What a Beautiful Mornin'," to the duo's "People Will Say We're in Love," they capture the magic of Rodgers and Hammerstein. Dramatic tension in *Oklahoma!* was provided by Rod Steiger, as the jealous and vengeful Jud. He goes so far as to torch the haystack that lovebirds MacRae and Jones are pitching woo upon.

***Oklahoma!* (1955) "All Er Nuthin'" with Gloria Grahame (RKO)**

**Gene, Gloria, J.C. Flippen, Charlotte Greenwood (RKO)**

Enter Gloria Grahame. Will Parker's romantic interest was the addle-brained Ado Annie, played by Grahame. She sports a secret smile during the number "I Cain't Say No," confessing to her flirtatious nature. Will isn't inclined (or capable) of admitting his own sexual predilections. Gene and Gloria's risqué duet "All Er Nuthin'" provides perfect comic relief. If they ever had a baby, he cautions her, "He better look a lot like *me!*" At one point, they emerge from a cornfield after sampling a bit of bliss. During filming, however, Gene wasn't exactly amused by Grahame. "She would do terrible things," he said, "She would step on my feet!"[188] Grahame went out of her way to upstage other cast members. Author Robert J. Lentz's bio on Graham indicates, "Gloria alienated everyone on the production with her behavior. It was her last major Hollywood role."[189] Nonetheless, Gene and Gloria's scenes together indicate that Will and Ado Annie are *right* for each other.

Grahame, who received second-billing, lacked the musical talent of the other players. She made it work to her advantage. Known for dramatic noir, Grahame earned an Academy Award for her role in *The Bad and the Beautiful* (1953). Even so, her off-beat casting in *Oklahoma!* (a role that Betty Hutton turned down) was a plus. Richard Rodgers insisted that she was perfect for Ado Annie.

Critics agreed. Author/critic William Zinsser praised, "Gloria Grahame steals the acting honors as Ado Annie … by underplaying the role. Her subtle performance is one of the movies' biggest treats."[190] Bosley Crowther for *The New York Times* noted, "Gene Nelson's lanky Will Parker is a deliciously light-footed, dim-witted beau to the squeaky and occasionally pretentious Ado Annie of Gloria Grahame." *Motion Picture Herald* declared Gene Nelson was "a dance triumph in less than his earned share of footage."[191] *Variety* concurred that *Oklahoma!* emerged as "a fresh, crisply acted and beautifully sung concoction … an outstanding box-office attraction."

*Oklahoma!* was filmed simultaneously in Cinemascope and the new 70mm process Todd-AO. The roadshow run grossed close to $9 million. The film was nominated for four Academy Awards, including Best Color Cinematography and Film Editing. It won for Best Scoring of a Musical Picture, and Best Sound Recording.

**Will rides the train (RKO)**

***Oklahoma!*** **(1955) original ad (RKO)**

<><>

In March 1958, Gene would repeat his role of Will Parker, Off-Broadway. The New York City Center Light Opera revival of *Oklahoma!* was sold-out during its two-week run, receiving unanimously affirmative reviews. *Variety* rated it "still fresh, vibrant and thoroughly enjoyable. Gene Nelson is doing a nifty job." The review rated Helen Gallagher's Ado Annie "right up her alley."[192] Original cast member Betty Garde was on hand as Aunt Eller. In July, Garde and Gallagher joined Gene for a two-week summer stock engagement of *Oklahoma!* in Denver.

***Oklahoma!*** **1958 revival: Gene, Helen Gallagher (Ado Annie) and Betty Garde (Aunt Eller)**

Gene's affection for *Oklahoma!* was underscored with a sense of humor. It was evident during a 1972 "Richard Rodgers Celebration," for the composer's 70th birthday. Before doin' some ropin' and singin' for the audience, Nelson mused, "I would like to give my impression of a 52-year-old man, giving his impression of a 35-year-old man, playing an 18-year-old cowboy."[193] Cowpoke Will Parker was ageless. Jumping ahead another decade, Gene (age 62) and Shirley Jones were invited to a Hollywood press preview for the 70mm restoration of *Oklahoma!* He told a reporter for *The Oklahoman,* "When they told me they were gonna open it in the giant Todd-AO screen again, I was thrilled to death. Shirley Jones and I attended a press screening, but there was no one else available from the cast, so there couldn't be a gathering of the clan. Shirley and I sat there and cried. It was so moving to see that picture in its original form."[194] As a member of *both* the National Film Society and the American Film Institute, Gene Nelson "took an active part in the acquisition of films for restoration and preservation."[195]

Shooting *Oklahoma!* was completed in December 1954. In January, Gene flew to London to film the British sci-fi, *Timeslip* (1955). The film was released in the U.S. as *The Atomic Man* (1956). Since the 1940's, the British film industry required their theaters to show a percentage of films *made* in Britain. To meet the quota, exploitation companies came to the fore. To get distribution in the U.S., they often hired American actors who would take lead roles for a small salary. Despite the salary, Gene's mother Lenore tagged along for this venture. It had been over two years since Gene's dad passed away. Once in London, Gene bought her a new mink coat![196] During their stay, wherever Gene went, Lenore went.

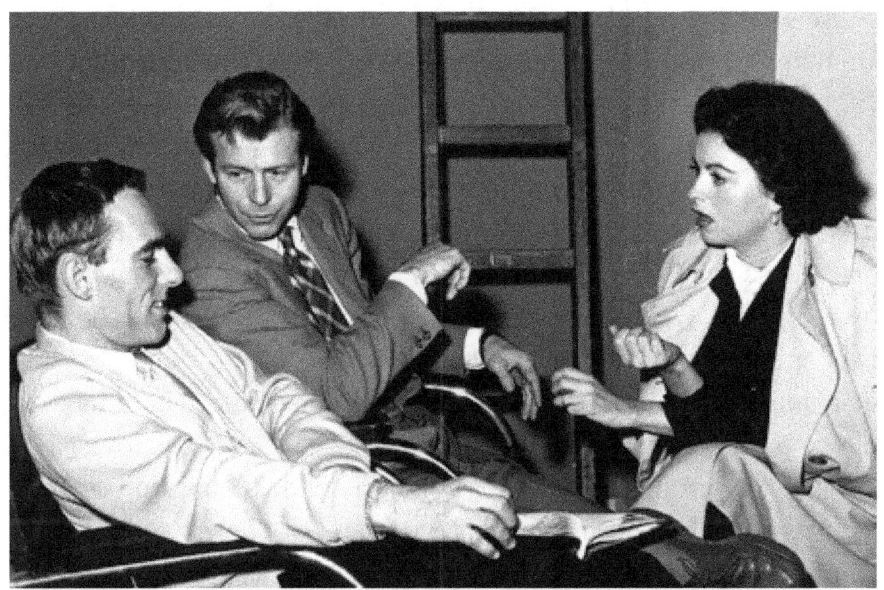

***The Atomic Man*** (1955) Director Hughes confers with Gene, and Faith Domergue (Todon)

In *The Atomic Man*, Nelson and fellow American co-star Faith Domergue team as reporters. They delve into mysterious circumstances surrounding a nuclear scientist who, after being pronounced dead, comes back to life. A clue to solving the mystery centers on the scientist's ability to answer questions seconds before they are asked. Domergue's photos reveal a glow emanating from his body. Gene follows his hunches … radiation poisoning. While investigating, Gene ends up with a bullet in his arm. Before he and Domergue discover the truth, they are side-tracked by the machinations of an Argentinian tungsten magnate determined to blow up the scientist's lab.

A preposterous scenario, but sci-fi films tended to use radioactivity as if it were a magic formula. The dangers of nuclear fallout were gaining visibility. The shaky, radioactive sheen that films perpetrated upon moviegoers would soon lose its power. None-the-less, *The Atomic Man* held viewers' attention. *Monthly Film Bulletin* praised *The Atomic Man* as being "quite a credible addition to the British school of scientific thrillers." Director Ken Hughes created just the right tempo and visual nuance while getting strong performances from his cast. Nelson is perfectly pitched to carry the necessary tension. Even as suspense builds, he deftly handles a dash of comic relief after being fired. He exists the boss's office, defensively spewing verbiage in self-defense. With documents clenched between his teeth, no-less, he tells co-workers, "Don't think it hasn't been fun, 'cause it hasn't!" An impossible task, but he pulls it off … before heading to the nearest pub.

By the time *The Atomic Man* was released in the U.S., fifteen of the original ninety-three minutes had been shorn. In 1996, Faith Domergue commented, "It had a very good director, Ken Hughes, and I thought it was a good film, though the pace was slow, *very slow*." She referred to the original version, *Timeslip*. In 2017, journalist Janne Wass, commented that *The Atomic Man*, "moves along at a good pace and is infused with snappy dialogue. It is well shot and beautifully lit. Nelson and Domergue do a great job in the lead roles. They have good on-screen chemistry."[197] While the film has its detractors, director Ken Hughes, who had focused mainly on crime dramas at this juncture, was pleased with it. Hughes would go on to receive wide acclaim for his *The Trials of Oscar Wilde* (1960) starring Peter Finch in the title (and controversial) role.

On March 25, Gene and Lenore were scheduled to return to the U.S. aboard the *Queen Mary* – traveling first-class. Instead of sailing from Southampton, Gene opted that he and his mother *fly* from London to New York.[198] He was eager to get back to the states. There was an offer for a Broadway show. Lucrative TV offers were also rolling in, one of which would team Gene Nelson with his next romantic attachment—a joyful affair that would last over a year, with … no strings attached.

When asked about Broadway shows that were offered him, Gene admitted, "They look pretty exciting, but a good leading role is hard to find … particularly in musicals. A *Pal Joey* role, a part with guts where you can really use your talent, doesn't come along very often. I *don't* understand Broadway and I don't pretend to, that's why I have to be so careful." Ironically, while in New York, Gene opted to film a "live" TV special for CBS' *The Best of Broadway*. The episode was an adaptation of the 1926 stage hit *Broadway* by George Abbott and Philip Dunning. Gene tackled a role originally played by the fast-talking wisecracker, Lee Tracy. As a clean-cut hoofer at a speakeasy, Nelson's character is intent on marrying a virtuous chorus girl (Piper Laurie). Complications ensue when a gangster rum-runner (Keenan Wynn) casts his eyes on her. Also on hand was Joseph Cotten, as a Broadway gumshoe (detective). The production was directed by Franklin J. Schaffner, who had recently won an Emmy for an adaptation of *Twelve Angry Men.* Things looked promising from the get-go, and Gene's decision to climb on-board made sense. Upon airing on May 4, critics blasted *Broadway* to smithereens. *Variety* said it had "none of the spark or fire of the original." The review rated the direction as "inept," and found Joseph Cotten "ludicrous," Keenan Wynn "uncomfortable," Gene Nelson "rather silly," and Piper Laurie? Well, she was rated "virtuous enough."[199]

**The Best of Broadway (May 1955) "Broadway" – with Martha Hyer, Joseph Cotton, Piper Laurie, Gene (CBS)**

The experience put Gene Nelson on the defensive. "You put on a TV show in less than two weeks' time," he pointed out, "and the critics review it as if it were a Broadway production. A legitimate show has weeks of preparation and then an out-of-town tour before it is reviewed. In TV there is none of that. I think TV people are miracle men to do so much in so little time."[200] If anything worthwhile came out of Gene's *Broadway* venture, it was the real-life, romantic bond with Piper Laurie. In her 2011 memoirs, Piper offered details about the production:

*Rehearsals were intense. I worked on my dance number with Gene, who also  choreographed. He was delightful, so sunny and cheerful and motivating. ... We had so much fun. I hadn't felt this light in a long time, and of course, we became lovers. Even after my parents arrived [in New York] I had decided  no more pretense. If they came into the bedroom while we were making love,  I would just deal with it.*[201]

Before going full-steam ahead with Piper, Gene flew back to London to film another British quickie.

<<>>

***The Way Out* (1956) Gene with Mona Freeman (Todon)**

*Dial 999* (1955) is considered by some to be the nadir of Gene Nelson's film career. Released in the U.S. as *The Way Out* (1956), Nelson finds himself covering up facts surrounding his (unintentional) killing of a bookie to whom he was heavily in debt. The confrontation took place at a bar. Upon arriving home in a drunken stupor, he tells his wife (Mona Freeman) that it was in self-defense—he is being framed. While Mona digs closer into the facts of her gambling, philandering husband, she falls for the detective investigating the case. What film critic Leonard Maltin christened a "BOMB," in all fairness, begins with an impressive "Bang!" The opening scenes grip the viewer's attention with a moody noir atmosphere. Nelson's frantic emotional state is spot-on. He finds no respite from his paranoia, but the script eventually lets him down as he attempts to smuggle himself out of the country. He and Freeman run out of steam. The focus turns to investigators chasing their own tail. During the proverbial climactic scene, Gene, caught in a frantic scuffle with police, is accidentally hit by a bus … thus providing him (and other cast members) "the way out."

British *Today's Cinema* gave the only positive nod to *Dial 999*, finding it to be a, "Very solid, and well-made thriller."[202] Across the pond, eleven minutes were cut. *Film Bulletin* rated *The Way Out* "a weak melodrama for double bills … mediocre and incredible." The review stated Nelson "isn't very believable," Freeman's delineation "stretches credibility," and Montgomery Tully directed "with a pedestrian touch."[203] *Variety* commented on Tully's "inept direction," and that Nelson's "scant acting ability makes a bad role worse." On that sour note, it would be another six *years* before Gene Nelson made another film.

<<>>

**Shower of Stars (June 1955) with Betty Grable (CBS)**

In Hollywood, Gene became more involved with television, working with and coaching such talents as Betty Grable and Shirley MacLaine. He taught dance classes for his old mentor Nico Charisse, and attended screenings for *Oklahoma!* Piper Laurie tagged along on numerous occasions. The duo did not go unnoticed. In the fall of 1955, Sheilah Graham was predicting marriage after seeing them "all lovey-dovey" at the star-spangled Hollywood premier of *Oklahoma!*[204] In her memoirs, Piper rhapsodized about Gene's "golden body …. beautiful smooth muscles. We slept all snuggled up and wrapped around each other. When I opened my eyes in the morning, this sunny golden boy was there smiling at me. It was like what a honeymoon should be. He was a superb lover."[205]

***Oklahoma!*** **premier – Gordon MacRae, Shirley Jones, J.C. Flippen, Sheila MacRae, Piper Laurie, Gene Nelson**

**Spring 1956 – with Piper Laurie**

**General Electric Theater (1955) "Tryout" – with Ann Harding (CBS)**

# Chapter 9

# Lights! Camera! Direct!

*"Acting, producing, and directing … If you're reasonably
intelligent and can do one, you can do the others"*
Gene Nelson (November 1955)

This quote from Gene Nelson was said shortly after he "directed"
cinema legend Ann Harding in *Tryout* for TV's *General Electric
Theatre*. Harding was a major star during Gene's youth. Her ethereal
edge in such classics as *Peter Ibbetson* (1935) opposite Gary Cooper,
had staying power. For *Tryout*, Harding was challenged with playing
an aging actress with poor eyesight, determined to make a Broadway
comeback. Gene was a young director confronted with Harding's
desperation. *Variety* noted, "the script didn't make many demands
on the cast. Miss Harding had the best role, and to her credit, did
nicely by it."[206] The review described Nelson as "merely looking
alternately bright and downcast."

Nevertheless, the opportunity to "direct" Ann Harding, motivated
Gene to consider *becoming* a director. It finally fell into place a
couple of years later, while he was laid up in the hospital, bedridden
for months on end. During recovery, producer Albert McCleery paid
Gene a visit. He told Gene that when he was able to walk again, the
official role of director was all his. Gene acknowledged McCleery as
"the man who turned the tide for me."[207]

<\>>

1956. While honing his acting chops in televised roles, Gene kept in
good spirits with the help of Piper Laurie. The twosome enjoyed

each other's company. Piper recalled, "Gene kept me dancing in the classes he taught. We rode horseback several times a week in the evenings … and finally Gene bought me my own horse, a gorgeous palomino I named Sunny." Piper felt that she and Gene had little in common artistically or intellectually, and that *she* took acting more seriously. For a surprise birthday party (March 1956), Piper wrote a six-character satire on an episode of TV's *Climax* in which Gene co-starred with Mary Astor. During "secret" rehearsals, Gene got suspicious of Piper's absences, and (according to Piper) had someone follow her. When Piper's former beau David Schine showed up, Gene made an effort to spy on the duo. Schine, a multi-millionaire, was aligned with Roy Cohn, chief counsel to Senator Joseph McCarthy, who had recklessly fueled the anti-Communist scare in the 1950's. Schine, who didn't like the idea of being photographed with a movie star, wanted Piper to return an expensive ring he had given her. She did. When she and Schine met at a restaurant, for closure, she noticed Gene peeking behind a potted palm at an adjoining table. It was at this juncture that Piper "no longer found Gene's jealous behavior amusing."[208] When it came to someone with a reputation like Schine's, Gene's so-called jealousy was more likely *concern* for someone he cared about.

Piper enjoyed her time with Gene's son. "I loved spending time with his little boy Chris, who was then about eight," wrote Piper. "I had fun with all of Gene's family, including Gene's mother, who was a perfect and sweet lady who made Swedish pancakes for us." When Miriam made headlines during her and Gene's final divorce proceedings (June 1956), Piper was at Gene's side. Headlines weren't pleasant. "Loved Widely, and Too Well," was the lead caption for *The New York Post.* The article indicated that Gene boasted about his "extra-marital escapades in front of his wife." Miriam testified that she had to take their son to a child psychiatrist, because Gene took Chris along on his dates. Miriam mentioned having to seek a doctor's care for her own emotional state.[209] No mention was made of Miriam's relationship with CBS executive producer Jack Meyers, with whom she had been "going steady" for two years.[210]

<<>>

As the "honeymoon" simmered down with Piper, Gene took the lead in the aforementioned musical *Pal Joey*. It ran for two weeks at La Jolla Playhouse. Then came another lead role in TV's *Schlitz Playhouse* (September 1956). The series attracted screen legends like Bette Davis, Irene Dunne, Myrna Loy, George Brent, Sylvia Sidney, Gene's former co-star Ann Harding, and James Dean. Gene opted for *Moment of Vengeance*, a Western drama co-starring Ward Bond and Angie Dickinson. He played a gunfighter who elopes with the eighteen-year-old daughter (Dickinson) of a cattle baron (Bond). The baron is not pleased. Afterward, Gene Nelson couldn't get Westerns out of his blood. Before long, he signed up for the feature film *Natchez Trace*, to be shot in Tennessee.

**Schlitz Playhouse (1956) "Moment of Vengeance" – with Angie Dickinson (CBS)**

Prior to heading to Tennessee, Gene signed on for *Foolin' Ourselves*. Intended for Broadway, the musical-comedy revue closed in January 1957, while on tour. *Variety* critiqued that Gene "came off well-enough, though given less to do than seems appropriate."[211] By May, Gene opted for another musical-comedy, *Darling I'm Yours,* which had a brief run at San Francisco's Curran Theatre. *Variety* thought it was filled with "misfired gags ... to an audience silence that was deafening." The review singled out Nelson, playing the suitor of a young Polynesian (Lisa Gaye), as being "something of an exception. Somehow, he achieves some empathy with the audience."[212]

Wayne County, Tennessee. In July, Gene arrived on location to film *Bandits of Natchez Trace.* The 1830's true-life saga detailed the machinations of a slave trader (Zachary Scott) who robs and kills travelers in the wilderness of Natchez Trace. Gene was assigned the role of the "good guy" who infiltrates the trader's cult-like followers and brings about their downfall. During rehearsals (August 5), Gene jumped a horse in a chase sequence. The horse suddenly reared up and fell backwards, landing on Gene, who ended up with a broken pelvis. He was hospitalized for eight weeks. The production went on without him. When he was able to return home, Gene was bedridden for another two months. "I now had to figure out what to do," he recalled. "I couldn't dance, even if there had been pictures to dance in."[213] In the meantime, Gene kept busy adapting novels into script form. That Fall, Gene sued Panorama Pictures for $75,000. The company had failed to comply with California workman's compensation laws. The sum reflected a combination of hospital bills and lost wages.[214] In many ways, the incident helped redefine the life of Gene Nelson.

<<>>

Producer Albert McCleery showed up while Gene was in the hospital. McCleery directed the first televised production of *Hamlet,* starring Maurice Evans and Ruth Chatterton. He also originated NBC's ambitious series *Matinee Theatre*. Gene had appeared in a segment titled *Fiddlin' Man*, as a medicine man in the wild west. As Gene Nelson laid there, bedridden, *McCleery* became the medicine man. "He gave me a show to direct," said Gene, "the Bret Harte story 'Prosper's Old Mother,' and that started me off as a director."[215]

Gene was in sync with America's obsession for westerns. As a director, he was off to a good start with *Prosper's Old Mother* (May 1958). The one-hour presentation (in color) was given a nod from a critic who found it to be "an amusing adaptation of Bret Harte's famous story."[216] The tale of a gold prospector who hires an elderly woman (Mabel Albertson) to be a surrogate mother for his fellow miners, was a popular one. It had previously been seen on *General Electric Theatre* starring scene-stealer Ethel Barrymore as the medicinal hooch-guzzlin' "ma."

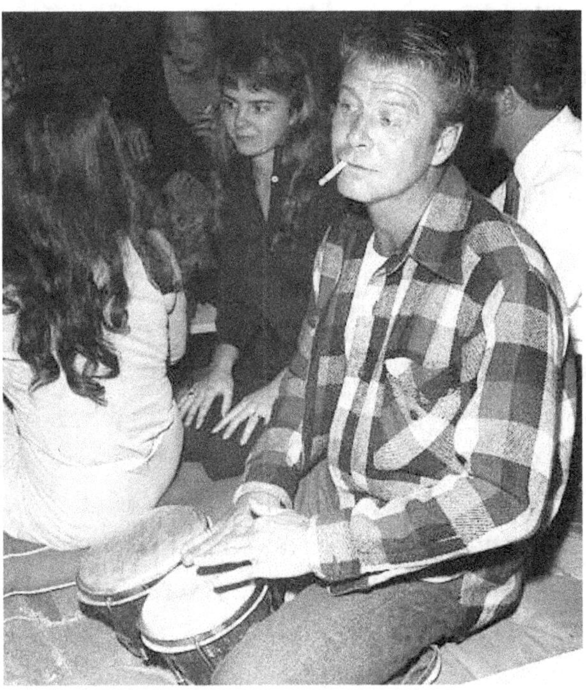

**1958 – Pandora's & Bongos – with Nina Foch, Albert McCleery, Reginald Gardiner**

When not working, Nelson and producer McCleery enjoyed hanging out with the "beat generation"—writers, artists and musicians who rejected the mores and materialism of conventional society. Soul-searching, rolling cigarettes and playing bongos, were part of the deal at Pandora's Coffee House on Sunset Blvd. It was around this time that San Francisco columnist Herb Caen coined the term "beatnik." While at Pandora's, Gene didn't sport a beatnik goatee, he simply headed straight for the bongos.

Following a full recovery, Gene signed on for an off-Broadway engagement of *Oklahoma!* The joy of dancing again was accompanied by cupid's arrow. Gene had fallen in love. Her name was Marilyn Morgan, age twenty-six, and she was employed by MGM as a studio secretary. On August 7, 1958, the couple were wed in Sherman Oaks at the home of Gene's friend and dance partner Pat Horn. Gene mused that being on crutches had not handicapped his pursuit of Miss Morgan. The couple had first met ten months earlier at a party in Beverly Hills. Columnist Mike Connolly threw the newlyweds a champagne wedding reception. Connolly, a friend of Marilyn's, hosted many such receptions over the years to promote his gossip column. Guests included Marge and Gower Champion, Jayne Mansfield, and pianist-composer Oscar Levant (all regulars at Connolly's soirees).[217]    Connolly reported that while on their "quickie honeymoon" Gene and Marilyn had won the first six races, *plus* the daily double at Del Mar racetrack.[218]

**August 1958 – Gene and Marilyn Morgan**

<<>>

Gene reflected in 1963, "Five years ago I realized I wanted to direct. Even before then, I had thought about it. I kept it to myself, in the back of my mind, until finally I openly resolved that this was what I wanted to do. All the time my interests were leading me to it. My stage work, dancing, acting, choreography."[219] For New Year's 1960, Gene directed *Our Musical Ambassadors* for *The Bell Telephone Hour.* Guests included trumpeter Louis Armstrong, and Gene's former co-star Shirley Jones. The Armstrong segment is truly a visual treat—lighting and camerawork capture the dynamic trio of Satchmo, his trumpet, and his handkerchief. A vocal quartet joins in for a nicely choreographed finish.

**Hit the Deck (Summer 1960) Producer Guy Lombardo faces: Gene, Jane Kean**

Summer of 1960. Gene took a break from TV. Guy Lombardo offered him the lead role of a philandering sailor in a revamped version Vincent Youmans'1927 musical-comedy, *Hit the Deck.* Jones Beach Marine Theatre (off Long Island) was the venue. For three months, Gene Nelson danced and crooned to Youmans' classic ballad "Time on My Hands." It was a real crowd-pleaser. According to *Variety*, after setting a new house record, *Hit the Deck* was held over.[220] Producer Lombardo and his Royal Canadian Orchestra, also helped to keep things afloat.

In October 1960, Gene choreographed and danced for a "live" *Hallmark Hall of Fame* presentation *Shangri-La'* (based on the James Hilton novel *Lost Horizon*). Journalist Walter Hawver praised its "soaring simplicity and immense beauty." A generous assessment. The show had flopped on Broadway in 1956, and the re-write for *Hallmark* ... wasn't much of an improvement. Amid mostly stark set designs and repetitious dialogue, Shangri-La's mystical emphasis on "being" as opposed to "doing," lacked delicacy. *Variety* summed it up as an "elaborate failure." Luckily, TV viewers were treated to an enticing *pas de deux* ballet "The Second Time in Love," which Gene choreographed for himself and Helen Gallagher. Hawver complimented their ability to be "perfectly natural" as a couple finding "a new lease on life."[221] Their dance provided lithesome respite from all the philosophizing. Claude Rains was on hand as the mystical High Lama.

Altogether there were ten Western-themed acting roles that Gene tackled between 1958-61—including a dramatic episode of *Rawhide* (October 1959), a series which made a star out of a young Clint Eastwood. *Incident of the Shambling Man*, starred Academy-Award veteran Victor McLaglen as an ex-prizefighter, and was directed by McLaglen's son, Andrew. Gene got to lock lips with Anne Francis, who played McLaglen's scheming, widowed daughter-in-law. She wants to put dad-in-law in an asylum. Gene sees through her ruse and together they get McLaglen "all riled up" in the center of town at an opportune moment. McLaglen unintentionally ends up socking Gene into the hereafter. By the end, Francis joins him. McLaglen himself died a month after the broadcast.

**Rawhide (1959) "Incident of the Shambling Man" Gene, Anne
Francis, Victor McLaglen (CBS)**

On the lighter side was *Law of the Plainsman* (May 1960). In *Trojan Horse*, Gene played a whip-twirlin' sharp-shooter in a Wild West show. He is dazzling to watch. For a fast buck, Gene comes to the aid of an Apache marshal (the charismatic Michael Ansara). While Gene's character sees himself as a confirmed coward, he transforms (convincingly) into a godsend for Marshal Ansara. Together they get the bad guys. Although the one-season series failed to develop a consistent tone, depicting a Harvard educated Native American in a lead role was a bold move for 1959-60. In the Fall of 1960, Gene filmed the lead role for a western pilot called *The Rambling Man*, but it was not picked up by major networks. Understandably, his resolve to direct came into full focus.

**The Rifleman - Gene Nelson directs Johnny Crawford and Chuck Connors (ABC)**

By October 1961, it was full steam ahead for *director* Gene Nelson. He headed West once again to direct episodes for the hugely popular, *The Rifleman*. Previous directors for the series had included Sam Peckinpah and Ida Lupino. Gene helmed eight episodes, by five different writers. The focus was on rancher Lucas McCain (Chuck Connors) and son Mark (Johnny Crawford), as they face compelling, ominous, and sometimes contrived situations. A tug at the heart was most always a fitting climax. McCain's sees himself as a "sodbuster," linked to the land, and content to be among regular people. Nonetheless, his suspicions about folks carry the necessary tension. The episodes that Nelson directed dealt with themes such as land-grabbing males, and (still relevant today) gunsmiths who will do anything to make a buck and sell their wares. Intermittent dashes of parental devotion and humor added to *The Rifleman*'s popularity. Gene's own expertise with horses offered a visual grip to their importance in the wild west. The real upshot for Gene Nelson at this juncture, was turning on his TV Monday nights to catch the satisfying sight of …

**The Rifleman (1961-62)**

**Buster around the time Gene "directed" him**

**Swanson on Burke's Law (1964) (ABC)**

**Elvis and Gene on the set of *Harum Scarum* (1965) (MGM)**

# Chapter 10

# Directing Buster Keaton, Gloria Swanson ... and Elvis!

Before immersing himself in directing, Gene took on two starring roles for the big screen. The low-budget features were produced by Robert L. Lippert's Associated Productions, Inc. (API). In 1961, Gene filmed the noir thriller *20,000 Eyes*—a six-day shoot. As a resourceful thief, he conspires to steal diamonds from a museum display. If successful, he'll be able to pay off a tough mobster. He is assisted by his girlfriend (Merry Anders) and their pal (James Brown). Gene's lithe, acrobatic ability makes the nighttime diamond heist a taut, visual experience. A New York critic observed, "Nelson is exceptional as the swindler."[222] *Variety* noted the "capable performances," and found the film to be a "competent ... superior quickie that will hold an audience between main courses."[223] *Boxoffice* indicated that while the cast would "set no marquees afire," they were "effective." Numerous plot twists toward the finish felt drawn out. API, however, was satisfied. Gene made another "quickie" the following month, in color. For this, he headed to Arizona.

***20,000 Eyes* 1961 (API)**

*The Purple Hills*, directed by Maury Dexter, was filmed near Phoenix. The action near Superstition Mountain, was captured in CinemaScope by the reliable lens of Floyd Crosby. Crosby had filmed Gary Cooper's award-winning performance in *High Noon* (1952). In *The Purple Hills*, Crosby's camera followed Gene Nelson, a lone drifter and veteran of the Civil War, as he arrives on horseback in Apache Territory. His motive? To be a one-shot bounty hunter. He succeeds. That is, until the outlaw's partner (Kent Taylor) wants to cash in. Gene nailed two knockout slugfests with Taylor. Amid the chaos, a band of Apache resolve his dilemma, slaying Taylor. Nelson then makes an unexpected about-turn. He leaves behind a $8,000 cash reward, and rides into the sunset with the dead man's young brother and his attractive guardian (Joanna Barnes). *Variety* assessed,

"The three stars dispatch their roles competently." The review noted that Crosby's photography gave "a special lift to the production … a satisfactory lower-berth western."[224] Even so, the script lacked the grit and dialogue to trigger what appeared to be a heart-felt, life-changing transition.

**The Purple Hills (1961) with Joanna Barnes (API)**

*The Purple Hills* was written by Russ Bender, who co-starred as the deputy marshal. In 2005, director Dexter referred to Bender as "my good friend, Russ Bender." Dexter added, "There wasn't *one single actor* that I worked with that I didn't *love*. And if I *ever* heard *any*body refer to them as has-beens, I'd do everything but hit 'em right in the mouth!"[225] In the *same* interview, Gene Nelson's name camp up. At that juncture, Dexter managed to put his foot into his mouth!

<><>

A dash of irony manifested after shooting *The Purple Hills*. Nelson's lawsuit against Panorama Productions finally came through. It had taken four years for a superior court judge to reward Gene's claim for lost wages: $72,675.[226] Unlike his character in *The Purple Hills*, he (understandably) accepted the reward. To his credit, he had completed several roles on horseback since his injury.

API then gave Gene an opportunity to direct. *Five Fingers of Death*, a seven-day shoot, began filming in May 1961. Upon release (March 1962), it was rechristened *Hand of Death*. John Agar starred as a scientist obsessed with developing a nerve gas that would banish the threat of nuclear war. He ends up like his toxic lab rats … a lumbering, charred beast. Everything he touches dies. There is no antidote. Agar's romance with Paula Raymond is doomed. Camerawork by Floyd Crosby moved the narrative along at a nice clip. *Motion Picture Exhibitor* nodded, "This program horror meller generates a fair amount of thrills and suspense, and is actionful [sic] throughout its brief running time." Years later, during an interview, Agar commented, "Speaking of Gene Nelson, *Hand of Death* was his first shot at directing, and I thought he did a very good job for his first go at it."[227] A year before his own death in 2002, Agar brought a copy of the much sought-after film to a party. His affection for the *Hand of Death* remained intact.

**The Hand of Death** **(1962) (API)**

In 2005, director Maury Dexter opted to gripe about Gene Nelson. After Gene got a few more films under his belt, he praised producer Robert L. Lippert, instead of Dexter, for giving him the opportunity to helm *Hand of Death*. Dexter, best known for horror films, indicated that *Hand of Death* was a "god-awful script" that he had *refused* to direct. Upon completing *The Purple Hills*, Gene, who was studying film at UCLA, approached Dexter about directing for API. A few excerpts from Dexter's tirade indicate what Nelson was up against.

> *I called Gene Nelson and I said, "Gene get your butt in here, I want to talk to you. I'm going to give you a script. It needs a lot of work." Well, he was elated ... the next morning he was there in the Lippert offices ... waiting for me! He had all these Mickey Mouse ideas. And, he improved it a little bit—not much, but a little! I went to Bob Lippert and told him, "I'm going to sign [Nelson] to direct ... I'll help him." Bob hemmed and hawed, but finally he said, "Okay, do it." So that's how Gene got the job. He took that little film of his and ... went to MGM and got a job directing a musical called Hootenanny Hoot (1963)! And then he did a couple more for MGM after that, a pair of Elvis Presley pictures!*

> *I'll tell you one thing that irritated me. An interview with Gene ... asked how he got started directing and he said, "Thank God for Bob Lippert! He gave me my first break. If it hadn't been for Lippert I would not be here today." That burned me up. I thought, "The least you could do, you son-of-a-bitch, is say, 'Maury Dexter got me the job.'"*[228]

Understandably, among Dexter's legacy of horror movies was *House of the Damned* (1963).

<<>>

Gene's most important production during his association with API, was a baby boy. Wife Marilyn gave birth to Douglas M. Nelson, on May 7, 1962. Gene and Marilyn were living in Encino. After Douglas turned two, Gene legalized his professional name. On June 16, 1964,

Marilyn appeared in a Los Angeles Superior Court for the procedure. She told the press they had contemplated the idea for some time, but "just now got around to it."[229] Marilyn, Douglas, and son Christopher (age 17) were also granted legal use of the Nelson surname. News items referred to Nelson as a "dancer-director."

Dancer-director Gene Nelson made his final film for API in 1963. It would be Nelson's last starring role for the screen. For this, he traveled to Puerto Rico. Producer Lippert hired twenty-six-year-old Jack Nicholson to write an original screenplay. Nicholson came up with a plot and bits of dialogue, and together with his friend Don Devlin, created *Thunder Island.* Nicholson intended to play the lead role. Lippert told Jack that he liked him better as a writer than an actor. Nicholson wasn't exactly a box-office draw.[230] His legacy of 12 Academy Award nominations were, at this juncture, beyond the horizon. *Variety* rated *Thunder Island* a "briskly paced … accumulation of suspense. By far the most convincing and colorful portrayal is that of Gene Nelson as the sadistic, raisin-eating, hired killer."[231] (Jack Nicholson, eat your heart out). On screen, Nelson, as Billy Poole, is hired to dispose of an exiled Latin American dictator living off the coast of Puerto Rico. Cool and dapper-looking, Poole arrives from the U.S. With the help of a liaison (Miriam Colon), he zeroes in on an American ex-pat (Brian Kelly), who delivers supplies to the despised dictator.

***Thunder Island* (1963) with Miriam Colon (API)**

When Colon attempts to explain her political motives, Nelson shrugs her off. His callous take on life is obvious. Incensed, she asks him, "Do you have any idea what it means to live under a dictator?" Nelson laughs, "You should have known my old man." Dashes of humor in the Nicholson-Devlin script do have bite. The subplot involves a tense reunion between Kelly and his wife (Fay Spain). Kelly sees himself as a victim of the American "rat race"—the almighty dollar and dictates of Madison Avenue. Using Kelly's wife as hostage, Nelson preps his scuba gear to sneak onshore. He asks Kelly, "Everyone relaxed? Thinkin' about hell?" However, once in "hell," Nelson's deadly bullet only wounds the dictator. Now *he's* the hunted man. *Variety* found the climatic chase scene, "excitingly mounted and filmed—the highlight of the picture." The camera lens of John Nickolaus Jr. was a key asset, along with Nelson's agile, athletic ability as he slithers through waves, and leaps across castle walls. And yes, Billy Poole is bumped off during the breath-taking finale. If anything, the script suggests the futility of employing guns and violence to change so-called humankind.

While trade publications rated *Thunder Island* a "good programmer"—audiences avoided the film. The tragic assassination of President John F. Kennedy that November, triggered an emotional response among Americans. Nicholson biographer Marc Eliot pointed out in 2014, "After Dallas, no one wanted to see a film about an assassination, and the film quickly disappeared from theaters."[232]

While at API, Gene began directing a marathon of scripts for the popular sitcom, *The Donna Reed Show* –22 episodes. Amidst Gene's association with Reed, she received the 1963 Golden Globe Award for "Best TV Star." Gene had the honor of directing guest star, and comedic mastermind, Buster Keaton in *Now You See It, Now You Don't* (1965). For this, Keaton was an accident-prone mechanic. Paul Peterson, who played Reed's son, recalled "watching in amazement" as Keaton put together the "skits" he was famous for. Most likely, director Nelson could only do the same.

Prior to directing Keaton, Nelson directed silent screen icon Gloria Swanson in *Who Killed Vaudeville?* (1964)—an episode of the tongue-in-cheek detective series *Burke's Law*. Gene was cast among the suspects as a vaudeville hoofer, thereby directing himself. Swanson's role was written for Mae West, who turned the opportunity down. Wearing a blonde wig, Swanson parodies West's voice, then dramatizes her final lines à la Norma Desmond—her character in *Sunset Boulevard* (1950). Gene Barry, as homicide investigator Amos Burke, zeroes in on hoofer Nelson as the prime suspect. The two engage in a dazzling fight at the Hollywood Bowl. One critic found "Who Killed Vaudeville?" to be a "corn-ball, but entertaining crime drama."[233]

**Burke's Law (1963) "Who Killed Harris Crown?" Gene with Gary Conway, Gene Barry, Ruth Roman (ABC)**

Gene's introduction to *Burke's Law* was in *Who Killed Harris Crown?* (1963). Again, he played the proverbial killer—a dance instructor. At a climactic moment, Gene throws a wild punch at Burke's young detective, Tilson (Gary Conway). While in orbit, Tilson takes a nose-dive into a swimming pool. Conway never forgot Gene Nelson! During a 2022 conversation with Gary, he told me, "Gene was an out-going, friendly guy. He created no tension on the set, no problems. Like having a best friend help you." During the run of *Burke's Law*, Conway worked with numerous directors. Gene Nelson stood out. "Gene was *very down to earth*," Conway emphasized. "Most of all, he was 'with it' all the time. As I think about him, I wish I had taken advantage of getting to know him."[234] Perhaps the two could have reminisced about their foray into 1950's sci-fi movies: Gene as *The Atomic Man* (1956) vs. Gary Conway as *I Was a Teenage Frankenstein* (1957).

Conway admitted that he didn't always recognize some of the screen legends that guest-starred on the series. One day he was waiting on the set, sitting next to another cast member. "There was this older guy," Conway told me. "We talked off and on for about forty-five minutes. Then we heard a voice announce, 'Mr. Rathbone, we're ready for you!' I had *no* idea. Producer Aaron Spelling created an amazing period getting them to come onboard." Gene himself would direct numerous classic film stars for television, including: Barbara Stanwyck, Robert Ryan, Ida Lupino, Ricardo Montalban, Anita Louise, Gene's former amour Jane Powell … and the perennial queen of Hollywood extras: Bess Flowers.

## M-G-M

It must have been a sobering experience for Gene Nelson to step upon the MGM sound stages—the studio that could easily have made him a major star fifteen years earlier.[235] Now he hoped to anchor himself as a *director* at a major studio. *Los Angeles Times* headlined, "Nelson Up a Rung on the Director Ladder."[236] By 1963, MGM was making one big-budget epic a year. *Hootenanny Hoot* definitely did *not* fall into that category. It was low-budget, cashing in on the folk-singing craze. A thin plot was amplified by the music of Johnny Cash, The Brothers Four, Sheb Wooley, gospel duo Joe and Eddie, Judy Henske, and George Hamilton IV singing his hit "Abilene." The film was produced by Sam Katzman, who helmed teenage exploitation films such as *Don't Knock the Twist.*

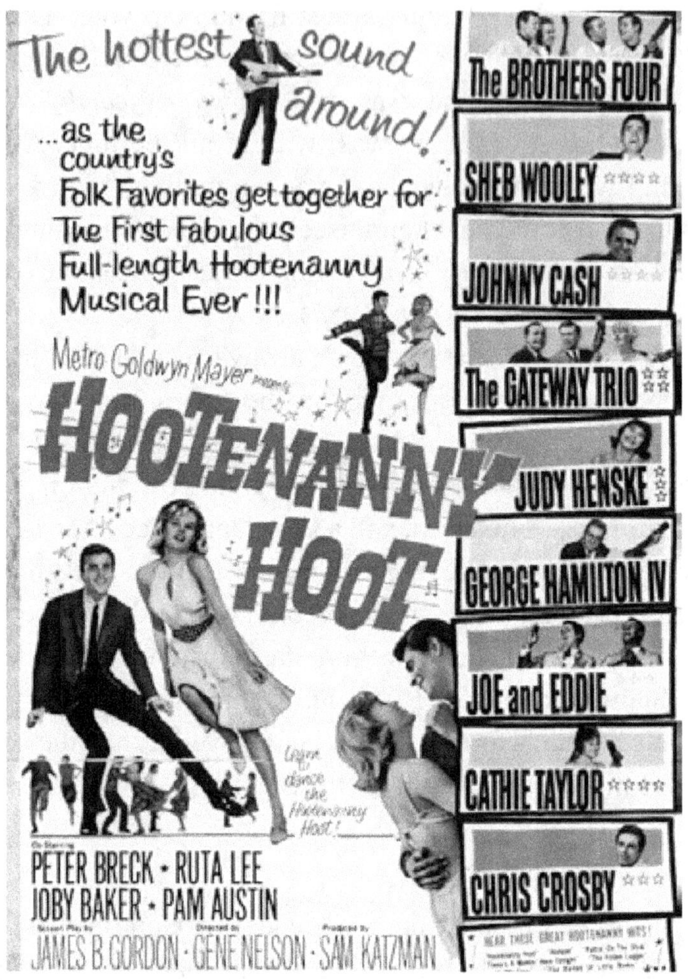


***Hootenanny Hoot* (1963) (MGM)**

In an interview with talk-show host Skip Lowe (1990), Gene mused: "I've gotta confess … the hootenanny era was kind-a weird. The picture was scheduled for nine days. I did sixteen pages a day. I used three cameras."[237] "Kind-a weird" describes the screenplay as opposed to the musical genre, but MGM got their wish—what *Variety* assessed as "a minor box-office bonanza." Adding, "The production is engineered at a snappy clip by director Gene Nelson."[238] In 1987, Johnny Cash was asked to comment about *Hootenanny Hoot*. His curt reply was simply, "Uh-huh. That was a movie I was in."[239] On screen, he simply mouthed his 1958 recording of "Frankie's

Man, Johnny." All the numbers were lip-synched. It sped up production. The script indicated there wouldn't be any "beatnik" types. NBC and CBS had blacklisted several folk artists. Social issues were themes folk singers focused upon. To avoid controversy, MGM quashed the participation of the genre's movers and shakers—Pete Seeger, Bob Dylan, Peter, Paul and Mary, The Kingston Trio, and Joan Baez. After the film's release, Bob Dylan, who had recently performed at a civil rights rally in Mississippi, gave a concert at Carnegie Hall. At one point the music stopped. For six minutes Dylan commented about the film, saying, "I went to see a movie called Hootenanny Hoot. Don't tell anybody. I don't want any of you to go see it." After describing the scenario, Dylan concluded, "Some of us, sometimes ... we just have to shake our heads."[240] In Hollywood, producer Katzman and MGM nodded approvingly as profits rolled in from *Hootenanny Hoot.* Gene Nelson was instantly awarded the honor of directing the "King of Rock-and-Roll" ... Elvis Presley.

Elvis Presley, it turned out, was a fan of Gene Nelson. Presley held fond memories from when he was seventeen, watching Gene's dazzling gymnastic dance routines in *She's Working Her Way Through College.* As shooting began on *Kissin' Cousins*, Presley quietly approached his new director. "Mr. Nelson," he said. "Hi Elvis, what can I do for you?" Presley asked, "I'm ... not bothering you, am I?" Gene detailed the encounter, years later.

*He would never call me Gene. It was always Mr. ... genteel and polite. I said, "Oh no, sit down." He said, "Do you remember coming to Memphis ... and you were riding in the back of a convertible Lincoln? And on the side, were banners that said, She's Working Her Way Through College?" I said, "That was when we were doing a PR*

*tour." Elvis: "You drove by the Memphis Theater. I was an
usher there. When I heard you were coming by, I ran out
of the theater. Stood on the curb." He went on and on and
I was getting embarrassed. How sweet of him.*[241]

Presley's manager, Colonel Tom Parker, was focused on making
money … and more money. After Gene helped complete the
screenplay for *Kissin' Cousins*, he sent a copy to Parker, who fired
back, "If you want an opinion … it will cost you an additional
$25,000."[242] Filming was on a tight schedule. Things got intense.
Elvis sensed that Gene was uptight. Gene later recalled, "Elvis came
to me the last week and he said he didn't like to work this way, it
wasn't worth it. He said he knew what pressure I was under and he
volunteered to get sick or show up late if it would help. I thanked
him and said to hang in—it was my problem not his."

In interviews with music critic Peter Guralnick, Gene fessed up
even further. "I had to really talk myself into liking that kind of
music. But if I was going to do this shit, you either fall in love with
it, or you don't do it at all—and I got myself very involved with
Elvis. I began to listen to him; I ran all his pictures. He was the
handsomest sonofabitch that ever walked across the screen. He
couldn't dance worth a shit, he really couldn't, but he had these
weird wiggles he produced, which was—okay."[243] Fans never tired
of Presley's mesmerizing "wiggles."

In October 1963, cast and crew headed east of Los Angeles to
Big Bear Lake and Cedar Lake, where the 1936 cinema classic *Trail
of the Lonesome Pine* was filmed. The log millhouse constructed for
*Trail …* served as home for the hillbilly family in *Kissin' Cousins.*
While *Trail …* told a story of the coal industry's intrusion upon
mountain folk, *Kissin' …* had the military grabbing land for a missile
base. Would Ma and Pa Tatum have to give up makin' moonshine?
Nephew Jodie (Elvis) confronts the army official in charge, a guy
named Josh Morgan (Elvis). "What are you doin' with my face?"
asks Jodie. Yep, Elvis played identical cousins. A clan of

"kittyhawks"—gun-toting, man-hungry gals—were on hand to make sure the "government critters" misbehaved. By the finish, moonshine guzzlin' was a-hummin' and missiles were reachin' for the sky. One kittyhawk would steal her director's heart a decade later … Maureen Reagan.

While one-note sex jokes saturate the film, the scenes with Ma Tatum (Glenda Farrell) and Pa (Arthur O'Connell) hold up best. Their down-home earthiness brought many a chuckle. Gene indicated that he enjoyed working with the "wonderful" Farrell.[244] No one was laughing, however, when she broke her neck! Glenda was required to flip Elvis over the front porch. She forgot to let go, landing on her head. She wore a neck brace for the remainder of the shoot.[245] Glenda's son Tommy Farrell was also in the cast.

***Kissin' Cousins* (1964) Arthur O'Connell, Glenda Farrell, Elvis (MGM)**

Gene stated that producer Katzman leaned "very, very hard. He was always on the set." Katzman was upset when Gene wrapped the film two days over schedule. The film grossed $2.8 million at the box-office. Presley's rendition of the title song reached #12 on *Billboard*'s Top 100. While *Kissin'* ... raked in the dough, Gene Nelson and Gerald Drayson Adams were nominated for the Writers Guild of America Award. Gene and Gerald wrote the screenplay. The award went to *Mary Poppins*. Reviews, for the most part, were lukewarm. *The New York Times* thought director Nelson had "limbered things up a bit," but that Presley's career had taken a "nosedive," adding, "Katzman's production is tired, strained and familiar stuff." *Variety* moaned, "What a mountainous waste of talent."

   *Kissin' Cousins* was completed in just over two weeks, at a cost of $800,000.[246] The budget was less than a half of Presley's previous films. Over $2 million had been spent on *Blue Hawaii* (1961), filmed in just over one *month*.[247] The Colonel, who lost millions at Las Vegas gambling tables, obsessed on profit, and producer Sam Katzman went along for the ride. Director Nelson deserved kudos for completing a next to impossible task. Perhaps Glenda Farrell summed up the backstory of *Kissin' Cousins* best, twenty-six years *prior* to the film's release, when her brassy blonde in *Golddiggers of 1937* lamented: "It's so hard to be good under the capitalistic system!"

**Glenda Farrell – *Golddiggers of 1937* (WB)**

<<>>

Many consider *Your Cheatin' Heart* (1964) the best of Gene Nelson's trio of MGM films. Aside from Katzman pounding his walking cane, Gene had to contend with the ex-wife of country singer Hank Williams. The biopic was intended for Elvis, but Audrey Williams didn't like the idea. She felt that superstar Presley was too much of a distraction. The lead went to actor George Hamilton. Hamilton headed to Nashville to meet Audrey. "I spent a month in Nashville drinking Jack Daniels with her," recalled Hamilton, "going out every night. Finally, she said, 'You're the only guy that's going to play this!"[248] George wouldn't have to sing a note. Audrey demanded that her fourteen-year-old son, Hank Jr., dub the vocals. She didn't stop there. She insisted that Williams' second wife Billie Jean be omitted from the script, and that there be no mention of Hank's divorce. On that note, director Nelson was handed a fictionalized account of a country legend.

***Your Cheatin' Heart* (1964) Gene, Audrey Williams, George Hamilton (MGM)**

On screen, audiences were transported to Alabama, where a youthful Hank learned guitar from an elderly African-American street musician named Rufus Payne. Director Nelson provides a touching look at a relationship that (according to the film) was at the core of Hank Williams. A scene where Rufus dies in Hank's arms, however, is pure fabrication. The film excludes Hank's mother, who was the real promoter for her son's talent—after he dropped out of school. Alcohol was also a problem for the teenager, as was stage fright. Omitting these "minor" details, the scenario jumps to 1943, when Hank meets Audrey. She allowed herself to be portrayed as a nag, relentlessly pushing Hank, who groans about "working night and day—reachin' for the almighty buck." Big money and popularity didn't curtail his binging. "My mind's too full!" he declares. At age twenty-nine, while being driven to a new gig, Hank Williams dies … the diagnosis: heart failure. While in transit to the gig, Hank opts to sing for local folk at a roadside stop. As he sings "I'm So Lonesome I Could Cry," he imagines his old mentor Rufus looking through the window. Hank Williams comes full circle, and easily pulls at the heartstrings.

Despite the liberties taken with Hank's life, critic Leonard Maltin recommends the film, adding that *Your Cheatin' Heart* contains, "One of Hamilton's best roles."[249] Hamilton reflected in his memoirs that producer Katzman, "cracked the whip, whacked the cane and the whole film was in the can right on time [13 days]. But he gave me free rein creatively and our director … Gene Nelson brought in something memorable, and even Sam knew it."[250] Indeed, upon release, *Motion Picture Exhibitor* found the direction "first rate."[251] *The New York Times* paid compliments to director Nelson for creating a film that was "quietly convincing every step of the way."[252]

<<>>

*The MGM Story* (1975) by John Douglas Eames, aptly summed up: "*Harum Scarum* had few rivals as the year's worst movie—more or less directed by Gene Nelson, and produced by mistake by Sam Katzman."[253] In mid-March 1965, production began on the fifteen-day shoot for *Harum* ... a musical spoof about a film star (Elvis) who visits the Middle East. His exploits on screen have been taken seriously by the Arabs. A bevy harems and relentless chase sequences discouraged Presley from the get-go. He lumbered along until filming wrapped. His attitude translated on screen. *The New York Times* groaned, "Mr. Presley wanders through *Harum Scarum* with all the animation of a man under deep sedation." Fact was, Elvis found solace while filming of *Harum* ... by studying meditation at the Self-Realization Fellowship in nearby Pacific Palisades. The Fellowship was founded by the late Hindu guru Yoganonda, who inspired a multitude of seekers searching for inner peace.[254]

After filming wrapped, Elvis apologetically signed a self-portrait to his director, saying, "Someday we'll do it right." For the time he spent with Elvis, Gene would reminisce, "I think he could have been a very good actor, but mostly he would just be his charming self and get away with it—because he was Elvis Presley."[255] As if being held hostage, Presley did as he was told. While *Harum* ... was a critical bomb, it was still a money-maker, earning $2 million at the box-office. The closing scene took place at a Vegas casino—Colonel Parker's playground—slot machines regurgitating jackpots. The Colonel's financial greed would continue to deflate his client's film aspirations.

<<>>

Following the reviews of *Harum Scarum*, Gene opted to return to TV, where he successfully jumpstarted the hugely popular, *I Dream of Jeannie*. One of the cast members, however, created such havoc and tension on the set, that director Gene Nelson was literally "fired" from the job, and withdrew from the limelight for several months.

**I Dream of Jeannie - Gene directs Barbara Eden and Larry Hagman (Yuma Beach, 1965) (NBC)**

# Chapter 11

# "Broadway, Beam Me Up!"

During the Fall of 1965, Gene headed to NBC to direct the premier episode of *I Dream of Jeannie.* The fantasy-comedy told the adventures of a 2,000-year-old genie (Barbara Eden) who pops out of a colorful bottle of Jim Beam bourbon, much to the surprise of a stranded astronaut (Larry Hagman). She falls in love, both saving and complicating his life. Producer/writer Sidney Sheldon hired Gene Nelson to direct, making it clear to cast members there would be *no* ad-libbing. Sheldon had won an Academy Award for Best Screenplay for the comedy classic *Bachelor and the Bobby-Soxer* (1947).

Filming began. Hagman didn't know his lines, and didn't care. Gene called Sheldon, announcing, "I'm quitting. Get someone else. Sorry."[256] Sheldon confronted Hagman with, "We have a tight schedule. We have a lot of pages to shoot every day. You'll say the lines exactly as they are written. Is that clear!" Hagman shrugged it off. Sheldon apologized to Gene, explaining there had been a "little misunderstanding. Will you give it another chance?" After a long pause, Gene replied, "I'll try." In his 2006 memoirs Sheldon notes that Hagman had emotional problems, being the neglected son of a Broadway superstar: Mary Martin. Things were okay until Gene couldn't get Hagman to come out of his dressing room one day. Hagman, who regularly imbibed champagne before going on the set, was sobbing. Sheldon advised Hagman see a psychiatrist. Gene later recalled, "When Larry got really mad, he'd go down to the set and piss all over. Eventually, NBC had to hire an on-the-set psychiatrist to be with him every day."[257] According to Barbara Eden, the psychiatrist advised Hagman to smoke pot.[258]

In his 2001 bio, Hagman put the blame on his director. "From the start we were like oil and water," wrote Hagman. "Gene misinterpreted my behavior as that of an ego-driven actor chasing stardom. But the cast knew better."[259] Oh, did they? In her 2011 autobiography *Jeannie Out of the Bottle*, Barbara Eden zeroed in on Hagman's abuse of drugs and booze, and his demanding personality. "It was clear that a showdown between Gene and Larry was imminent," she wrote. "Unbeknownst to me, Larry decided to precipitate that showdown by issuing an ultimatum to Sidney [Sheldon], 'Either Gene goes or I do.'"[260] When Sidney asked Eden if they should let Hagman go, she, not knowing what was really going on, told him that it would be a "big mistake" to replace him. Sheldon's ruse worked, much to Eden's dismay. She elaborated,

> *Before I knew it, Gene was out the door ... during the short period in which he directed the show, he stamped his indelible imprint on it. His contribution should never be underestimated. ... He never forgave me for siding with Larry, which is how he saw it, and he never talked to me again. Larry had gotten what he wanted.*[261]

No folding of her arms and blinking her eyes (a gimmick that Gene came up with) could alter the situation. Decades later, producer Sheldon, who had written eighteen novels in the aftermath of ... *Jeannie*, concocted a story that he fired Gene for yelling at an elderly prop man, who forgot to bring a persimmon to the set. Sheldon added that Gene "got along fine" with all the actors in the cast.[262]

Adding a little humor to the situation was Gene's pal from *This is the Army*, Hayden Rorke. Rorke's romantic partner, Justus Addiss, had also toured in the Berlin musical. Sidney Sheldon and Gene were pleased with Rorke's audition for the role of Dr. Bellows, a psychiatrist who questions the sanity of astronaut Hagman. "He had this pseudo-sophistication that I just loved," said Gene. "He and Jus Addiss had lived together for over twenty years. They were a pair.

Jus was very straight acting. Never in a million years would you know he wasn't straight. Hayden could slip into … this marvelous English manner, so he could get away with a little fey gesture. I don't think most people knew he was gay."[263]

Barbara Eden truly appreciated Gene's "inventive ways" in disguising her pregnancy while filming eight episodes. "Gene's wife, Marilyn, threw a baby shower for me," acknowledged Eden. That said, Gene Nelson took a few months off to regroup. After son Douglas turned four, the Nelson family relocated to Sherman Oaks. They lived next door to *American Bandstand* producer Dick Clark. Other neighbors included Henry Fonda. Then, on September 22, 1966, Douglas welcomed a little sister, Victoria Leandra Nelson.

In the Summer of 1966, Gene decided, once again, to direct for the big screen—at his old home base, Warner Bros. The youth-oriented flick, *The Cool Ones* (1967) was a light-weight satire involving a wannabe teen idol (Debbie Watson, in a role Nancy Sinatra turned down), heading to Palm Springs to jumpstart her career. A kooky talent-agent (Roddy McDowall) comes to her rescue, almost. McDowall's character was a parody of record producer/millionaire Phil Spector. While on location in Palm Springs, Gene took full responsibility as cast and crew boarded the Aerial Tramway to Mount San Jacinto. *The Desert Sun* reported, "Nelson ordered a supply of oxygen for a group of dancers … 8,500 feet up."[264] Due to the elevation, Gene encouraged dancers to use portable oxygen tanks. Safety for his team of players was first and foremost.

*The Cool Ones*, aside from Debbie Watson spraining her ankle, was completed without a hitch … that is, until the critics got hold of it. The film was produced at a Warner "B" movie unit, by actors William Conrad and Jimmy Lydon (co-producer). In author Charles Tranberg's absorbing biography of Conrad, he interviewed Lydon, who readily admitted, "Bill and I thought *The Cool Ones* had great potential, but it just didn't jell. Roddy did the best he could, as did our director, Gene Nelson ... but the picture didn't go anywhere. The kids didn't come—nobody came."[265]

***The Cool Ones* (1967) Roddy McDowell (WB)**

Veteran critic Bosley Crowther, for *The New York Times*, groaned, "I venture to guess that this will disgust even the kids."[266] *The Cool Ones* flopped at the box-office. Critic Leonard Maltin later summed up, "Embarrassing on all counts." Floyd Crosby's photography, and actor McDowall's parody of Phil Spector, were the only highlights. Prior to the release of *The Cool Ones*, Gene trekked over to Universal to direct Pat Boone for the TV-pilot *The Perils of Pauline* (1967). After two weeks of shooting, he dropped out due to "creative differences." Surprisingly, the first three episodes would be compiled into a feature film. As for *The Cool Ones*, this author came across no instance of Gene ever mentioning it.

Discouraged? Not Gene Nelson. Such setbacks would eventually push him toward another major transition ... Broadway. In the interim, Gene directed a TV pilot for Alan Alda, *Where's Everett?* No one cared. Gene then jumpstarted a series (that sold) for comedienne Phyllis Diller, *The Pruitts of Southampton*—an amusing, if predictable, romp with racy asides. In the first episode Diller, recalling the wedding of a relative betrothed to a nudist, was endowed with the line, "I'll never forget *his* side of the family!" Numerous other shows preoccupied director Nelson during the late sixties, most significantly, eighteen episodes of the immensely popular crime drama *The Mod Squad.* The series, about young, hip, undercover detectives, would be nominated for six Emmys, and four Golden Globe awards. The groundbreaking show dealt with racism, the anti-war movement, veterans with PTSD, sex-education, gun control, and the illegal drug trade. In her 2007 memoir, series star Peggy Lipton pointed to Gene as being one of the cast's favorite directors.[267]

**Mod Squad (1969) Gene directed "Keep the Faith" – with Sammy Davis Jr. and the squad: Michael Cole, Clarence Williams III, and Peggy Lipton (ABC)**

After a three-year sabbatical from acting, Gene opted to play a WWII vet in the long-running crime-drama *Ironside.* In *Tagged for Murder* (October 1967) he feared for his life. His squadron in Northern Italy had invested loot from a war-time bank heist into a Swiss account. Now, one-by-one, they were getting bumped off. As expected, police consultant Raymond Burr "irons out" all the clues, zeroing in on the real culprit. In 1973, Gene would direct a chilling episode of *Ironside* involving the supernatural. While Gene directed seven episodes of *The F.B.I* (1967-1970), son Douglas Nelson made his own acting debut (an uncredited walk-on) for the series. The seven-year-old was seen in the episode *Target of Interest* (directed by William Hale).

<<>>

**Star Trek - "Scotty, beam us up!" (NBC)**

**Star Trek (1969) "Gamesters of Triskelion" – William Shatner and the brains (NBC)**

"Scotty, beam us up!" Director Nelson helmed the first episode of *Star Trek* to use this popular catchphrase (often misquoted). Producer John M. Lucas (stepson of director Michael Curtiz) was pleased with Gene's handling of *Gamesters of Triskelion*—a six-day shoot.[268] The storyline told of aliens who abduct Captain Kirk (William Shatner) and two other crew members. They arrive on the planet Triskelion, where they become slaves, forced into the bloody art of being gladiators. The ensuing fight-to-the-death sequences are for their abductors' amusement. Triskelion is ruled by three brains encased in a glass dome (a metaphor for a mega-computer). The "violence as entertainment" theme aptly reflects our own toxic computer-driven world. As *Star Trek*'s Leonard Nimoy said of Triskelion decades later, "If you're thinking that this sort of notion has no relevance in today's society, think again. Or, just turn on a football game this Sunday."[269]

**Directing *Wake Me When the War is Over* (1969) (ABC)**

Aside from regular TV fare, Gene helmed TV's *Movie of the Week* (ABC). He was both behind the camera and co-produced *Wake Me When the War is Over* (1969). The WWII comedy centered on a naïve American airman (Ken Berry) stranded in Germany. He is taken in by a wealthy countess (Eva Gabor) who waits five years before telling him the war is over … she has fallen in love. For the most part, it was a case of "wake me when the movie is over." Leonard Maltin rated the one-joke offing: "fair." In late 1970, after Gene finished directing episodes for *The Mod Squad*, and Burt Reynolds' *Dan August*, he negotiated a *withdrawal* from any further TV commitments. Broadway had offered director Gene Nelson a starring role … as a dancer!

## Follies

"I thought it was time to shake my life up a little bit," Gene told talk-show host Merv Griffin.[270] Gene recalled listening to Gregory Peck reciting playwright Moss Hart. Hart encouraged others to (as Gene put it), "shake your life up … change things … don't become stagnant." "It kind of stuck with me," Gene told Griffin. "It came in handy when I got the call to come and do *Follies.*" After signing with producer/director Hal Prince (November 1970), Gene headed to New York. Rehearsals for *Follies* began in January. "It's pretty exhilarating for a guy my age, fifty-one—to know he can still hoof and carry a tune," Gene admitted. Not that he didn't have to get in shape. He arrived at the theater an hour before rehearsals began, to warm up. Gene explained:

> *I gave it everything I've got. When I went to the rehearsal hall, I couldn't lift a leg. But upstairs in the brain, I was telling myself, damn it, I'll conquer this. I attacked the problems with every fiber of my being. There was pain. Progress was slow. But I was determined to build up my muscles. Eventually, the stamina flowed back, and I knew my own power.*

Gene became aware, not so much of his brain, but of his inner *presence*—his ability to let go of self-doubt. He explained further:

> *People who lean on the church are using psychic crutches. I'd rather worship myself. The human mind and the human body are fantastic courses of physical and mental strength, rarely tapped to the maximum. ... I'm concentrating on the fact that I've turned back the clock. It's like starting life all over again.*[271]

As Gene focused on the moment at hand, things fell into place. *Follies* had its tryout (February 24-March 20, 1971) at the Colonial Theatre in Boston. Before long, Gene Nelson headed not only to Broadway, but a nomination for a coveted Tony Award.

**Follies (1971-72) Gene Nelson as Buddy**

Choreographer (and co-director) Michael Bennett created an athletic, "swing-around-the-pole" routine for Gene, titled "The Right Girl." His character Buddy, like other cast members, thinks too much about the past. When lyrics fail to express Buddy's true feelings, he breaks into a dance, mirroring something deeper. He swung around poles. He leaped upon furniture. Arabian cartwheels and double pirouettes underscored emotions. Inevitably, the six-minute routine brought down the house—a real showstopper, but not on opening night. Gene had injured himself during previews at the Winter Garden Theatre. In 2020, Bob Avian, who assisted with the choreography, noted, "It was a tough time for Gene; one of his sons in California was in a very bad accident, and Gene was, understandably, highly distracted."[272] Marilyn called to say that Douglas, age 9, had been hit by a truck. A brain injury put him in a coma, unable to talk. Marilyn encouraged producer Prince to keep Gene occupied with the show.[273] Gene kept bursting into tears during rehearsals. A month after the play opened, Douglas was making rapid recovery at New York University Hospital. Marilyn had located a posh apartment near Fifth Avenue. The family would stay in New York for over a year.

Inspired by Sondheim's love of old movie musicals, *Follies* focused on middle-aged show people, who gather for a nostalgic, boozy (and confrontational) evening as their beloved old theater is about to be torn down. Gene was assigned the role of Buddy, a traveling salesman, married, but with a girlfriend on the side. In his 2005 tome to *Follies*, production assistant Ted Chapin wrote that Nelson was, "quick and cheerful, always with a handshake … he and Buddy were a neat fit. He was clearly psyched for this experience … looking trim and fit."[274] Producer Prince cast people whose personal showbiz journey reflected aspects of the characters they were to portray. "We just kept hoovering up people who were close to the story," explained Prince.[275] Legends such as Gene, Alexis Smith, Yvonne DeCarlo, and Dorothy Collins, encouraged audiences to believe that they were just "playing themselves." Collins played Gene's wife, Sally, who is still in love with an old beau. Gene's other knockout number was, "The God-Why-Don't-You-Love-Me Blues." A talented cast zeroed in on the not-so-pleasant emotional snarls of romantic love. *Time* magazine summed up, "At its best moments—it is the most imaginative and original new musical that Broadway has seen in years." Despite opening to mixed reviews, both raves and pans,

*Follies* chalked up 522 performances—running from April 4, 1971 to July 1, 1972.

***Follies* stars: Yvonne De Carlo, Gene Nelson, Dorothy Collins, Alexis Smith, John McMartin**

In January 1972, a poll taken among editors and columnists, awarded Gene Nelson and Ruby Keeler (who was starring in a Broadway revival of *No, No Nanette*), plaques for being among the "six top motion picture dancers of all time."[276] New York Drama Critics named *Follies* the best musical of 1971. In April 1972, *Follies* was nominated for eleven Tony Awards, winning seven. The awards took place at New York's Broadway Theatre, hosted by Henry Fonda, Deborah Kerr, and Peter Ustinov. Sondheim won for "Best Original Score." Alexis Smith won for "Best Actress in a Musical." Gene was on board as "Best Performance by a Featured

Actor in a Musical," but lost to Larry Blyden in a revival of *A Funny Thing Happened on the Way to the Forum.*

In 2023, *Follies* co-player Michael Misita reminisced, "Gene and I had an affinity for one another due to both of us being dancer/actor/singers. Gene was a very genuine, unpretentious, extremely hard-working guy. I admired him and loved him for that. I learned a great deal listening to him. We both had a similar work ethic of being hard-working perfectionists. I'll always treasure being in the show *Follies* with this wonderful man."[277] After *Follies* closed, Gene and other cast members offered a reprise in St. Louis. Heading to Los Angeles, they headlined Century City's newly constructed Shubert Theatre (July 22-October 1). Hal Prince had visions of making an MGM film version, with Gene repeating his role on screen. Prince's press agent, John Springer, later claimed that Hal had a quarrel with someone at MGM, and dropped the project.[278] Prince claimed that the film was dropped due to apathy. Nevertheless, he hired someone to write a screenplay. In 2019, BBC Films would finally secure the rights to Sondheim's *Follies.* Dominic Cooke, who directed a 2017 production of *Follies* at London's Royal National Theatre, was set to direct. As of 2023, it's still a question of "wait and see."

As Gene, Marilyn, Douglas and Victoria settled back into their Beverly Hills residence, Doug returned to Rodeo Elementary School. Gene returned to directing, but still had theater in the back of his mind. In early 1973, he directed two segments of the TV movie *The Letters*—three letters, to be exact, which are delivered a year too late. Behind the camera, Gene lensed a sensitive performance from Jane Powell, and a dynamic portrait of a domineering matriarch from Barbara Stanwyck. Gene himself, got in front of the lens for the series *Circle of Fear*, as Janet Leigh's psycho, bug-collecting husband in *Death's Head.* She obtains a witch's potion to get rid of him. After his demise, as one critic put it, Leigh "looked particularly ludicrous as she swatted at the invisible bugs" who were avenging her dead husband. Even so, one couldn't look away![279]

**Directing Jane Powell and Barbara Stanwyck in *The Letters* (1973) (ABC)**

**Circle of Fear (1973) "Death's Head" Gene with Janet Leigh (NBC)**

Director Nelson kept busy with popular series such as *The Rookies, Cannon,* and *Barnaby Jones.* Actor Nelson supported Cloris Leachman in her Emmy-winning performance, *A Brand New Life.* Dancer Nelson was unexpectedly summoned back to Broadway, with top billing. Dan Dailey had broken his leg.[280] The former 20th Century-Fox dancer fell during rehearsals for *Music! Music!*

—which was about to open at City Center 55th Street Theatre. Taking on a lead role at the last minute showed what a trooper Gene was.

***Music! Music!* (1974) Gene, Larry Kert, Karen Morrow**

***Music! Music!* (1974) Gail Nelson, Larry Kert, Karen Morrow, Robert Guillaume, Donna McKechnie, Gene**

*Music! Music!* —a cavalcade of songs echoing back to 1895, ran for five weeks (April-May 1974). Gene danced, sang, and acted as master-of-ceremonies, using a narrative created by lyricist Alan Jay Lerner. "His dancing shouts for itself," cheered critic Jack O'Brian after seeing what he deemed "a warmly nostalgic show." Critic William Glover capsulated, "The solo opening entry by Gene Nelson, who emcees, tosses in a neat soft-shoe routine, jumps through a cowboy lasso and contributes some husky vocals."[281] Gene reprised his routine from *Oklahoma!* His soft-shoe number was to 1925's "Yes Sir, That's My Baby!" Despite a scathing review from *The New York Times*, *Time Magazine* cheered *Music! Music!* had "looted" popular tunes for a "delightful musical blowout."

When an intended tour of *Music! Music!* fell through, Gene headed back to California and … divorce. After almost 16 years of marriage, Gene and Marilyn parted ways. At this point in his career, Gene was unlikely fodder for gossip columns. Details of his split with Marilyn were not made public. It was also around this time that Gene and his eldest son Chris formed The Nelson Production Co. to develop properties for both film and television.[282] Chris eventually became a film editor, "the best editor in the business" according to his mother Miriam.[283] Shortly after Chris had turned twenty-one, he married his girlfriend Denise (May 18, 1968). Grandsons Christian, Josh and Matthew soon followed.

Autumn 1974. Gene jump-started the series *Get Christie Love!* The crime-drama detailed challenges faced by an African-American female detective (Teresa Graves). It didn't last long. Graves insisted on having Jehovah Witness advisors monitor the scripts. Viewers were not converted. The series was cancelled. The good news was, Gene had been selected to co-star on Broadway with classic cinema's Alice Faye. The nostalgia craze generated by producer Harry Rigby's *No, No, Nanette*, starring Ruby Keeler, prompted Rigby to ask Alice about touring in a revamped version of 1927's *Good News*. Faye, who was prone to stage fright, responded, "Oh, my god, I'd die!"[284] She relented only after Rigby agreed to ask her former co-star, John

Payne, to play opposite her. The two hadn't seen each other for seventeen years.

Over the next year, Alice gained confidence. Reviews were kind. Audiences enthusiastic. Being a fan of Alice Faye, I eagerly awaited her appearance at San Francisco's Curran Theatre (May 1974). *Bay Area Reporter* nodded, "Miss Faye can still tear your heart just by standing still and huskily crooning 'Together,' or throwing a mean bump in 'I Want to be Bad.'" The critic admired Faye and Payne's sense of comedy, summing up, "These two are not relics of a bygone era, but as vital and talented today as they ever were."[285] I brought a record album backstage for Alice to sign. Waiting in a long line behind her entourage of fans, I glanced over at John Payne, who gave me a knowing smile. He nodded his head toward Alice, acknowledging that *she* was the main attraction. I could tell that Payne was pleased as punch; no ego involved. He was happy for her. While Alice quickly signed my album, I managed to compliment her wonderful voice, and films I could watch over and over again.

*Good News* (1974) Stubby Kaye, Alice Faye, Gene Nelson

Towards the end of the tour, a critic for *The Los Angeles Times* put a damper on things. Changes were made, songs replaced, along with the director. During the reshuffle, Payne's contract expired. His leg was giving him problems. Producer Rigby, after considering Don Ameche and Van Johnson, decided that Gene Nelson would be a perfect fit. After opening at the St. James Theatre on December 16th, *The New York Times* noted, "Miss Faye is not the most animated leading lady … but her light baritone voice is pleasing, and she unquestionably dances with the guts of a Ruby Keeler. Gene Nelson … has less to do, but can still dance with panache (watch the guy's butterfly jumps) and has enormous personal charm and stage professionalism."[286] Gene later commented, "I didn't have a hell of a lot to do. Two weeks and we were closed." On January 4, 1975, after sixteen performances, came the final curtain. At this juncture, Gene, not having "a hell of a lot to do," shook his life up a little more. He began dating the rebellious daughter of California governor Ronald Reagan.

*Gene 1990*

# Chapter 12

# Always Giving

**"Not perfect, not always there, but always giving of himself ... 100%"**

*–Victoria Nelson Gordo*

"Maureen Reagan Dates a 56-year-old"—headlined a gossip column in August 1976.[287] At that time, Gene and his movie camera accompanied Maureen, Ronald and Nancy Reagan and their eighteen-year-old son Ron, to the GOP convention in Kansas City. While Gene lensed some of the proceedings, Reagan tried to win the Republican nomination for President. He lost. Maureen, who drifted in and out of her father's life, was onboard to support his campaign. Gene tagged along to support Maureen. The two also traveled together promoting the Equal Rights Amendment. Gene reflected in 1988, "Maureen offered to do anything she could for her father's presidential campaign, despite real political disagreements with him, especially on the subject of the Equal Rights Amendment. She came right out and asked him why he was so against women ... he was intimidated by her knowledge of the issues."[288]

Maureen, at this juncture, had also chalked up two marriages. One was brief, but brutal; the second ended when "they no longer found each other interesting."[289] Prior to Maureen's attempts at matrimony, Reagan (with the help of his pal, J. Edgar Hoover) had FBI agents investigate her romantic life.[290] Unsurprisingly, Reagan did not approve of Maureen and Gene's relationship. Between marriages, Maureen made a brief foray into film-making. Gene directed her two films: *Hootenanny Hoot* and *Kissin' Cousins* (in which she was one of rebellious Kittyhawks).

***Kissin' Cousins*** **(1964) Maureen Reagan (far left) (MGM)**

By 1975, Gene and Maureen reconnected and were living together. Gene recalled that Maureen "was a pain-racked lady who did not deserve the rotten things that had happened to her. … Nancy refused to see or speak to her for years on end. … I can't describe to you how Maureen would cry at night. So, she set upon trying to heal the family wounds as Nancy and Ronnie were gearing up for the big race in 1976."[291]

To create the image of a "united family," Nancy relented, inviting stepdaughter Maureen and Gene to dinner at the Reagan residence in Pacific Palisades. Gene reflected on the humor and pathos of the so-called "family reunion":

*God! What a night that was. Ronnie answered the door and immediately started playing the drunk scene in* She's Working Her Way Through College—*the Warner Bros. movie we had been in together in 1952. He was a lousy drunk, but he started his routine the minute he opened the door. He didn't even say hello to Maureen, but she pretended not to notice. That's how desperate she was to be accepted. Nancy and Ronnie were very lovey-dovey throughout the evening. Unnecessarily so. ... Maureen offered to do anything she could for her father's presidential campaign.*[292]

**1976 - A "dysfunctional family reunited" – Nancy, Ronald, Michael, Maureen, Ron Jr.**

As Reagan got in gear again to win the Republican nomination for President, his son Ron Jr. made it clear that he intended to have a career in ballet. He had dropped out of Yale to pursue his dream. Gene detailed, "Ronnie told me that Nancy … didn't want her boy dancing with homosexuals. She was more of a bigot about the homosexual thing than Ronnie was. After our talk, I strongly recommended that he and Nancy support their son, financially and emotionally."[293] Gene arranged for Ron Jr. to audition at the Stanley

Holden Dance Center in Los Angeles. Unmoved, Ronnie and Nancy declined to support their son. Stanley Holden gave him a job as a desk clerk to pay for his lessons. Afterwards, Ron Jr. joined the Joffrey Ballet. In 1980, *Time* magazine detailed, "It is widely known that Ron's parents have not managed to see a single ballet performance of their son, who is clearly very good."

While they were living together, Maureen came to Gene's rescue after he had a stroke. She went so far as to borrow $10,000 from her father to help with Gene's rehabilitation.[294] In the aftermath, Reagan's attorneys charged Maureen $481.00 interest on the loan. The last mention of Maureen and Gene in news columns was their appearance as judges at a Miss Apple Valley contest in May 1978. No details as to why they split up. In 2005, Michael Reagan was contacted by writer Frances Ingram, who was working on a career article about Gene Nelson. She asked if he cared to comment about his late sister's relationship with Gene. Michael replied, "When Merm was with Gene she was truly the happiest ... I am sorry that the relationship ended ... he was the best thing that ever happened to her."[295]

In 1988, Gene provided interviews for author Kitty Kelley's controversial *Nancy Reagan: the Unauthorized Biography* (1991). Upon the book's release, Gene told a reporter for *Time* that Kelley was "a master of embroidery" (no specifics). Nevertheless, Gene's observations about Reagan and company, are consistent in both tone and credibility.

<<>>

In the Fall of 1977, while directing a series for ABC, Gene met a young graduate from San Francisco State. Her name, Jan Wahl. Wahl was working as a stage manager for the studio, a role she had served during the 1977 Oscars. She was also busy being a documentary producer. A star-struck, classic movie fan, Jan was smitten with Gene, and vice-versa. They dated frequently. In 2023, the Emmy-winning Wahl enthused, "It was wonderful being with

Gene. I have fantastic memories. He was so sweet and smart." Like Piper Laurie, Wahl was forthcoming about Gene's skill as a lover, saying, "He *really* liked women. Gene was very much a woman's man. I can't say womanizer, because when he fell hard, he fell hard. He was kind and good. He was very sensual." Wahl was also entranced by Gene's professional skills. "He had tremendous talent. He was a good cutter. I sat with him cutting and editing at ABC. He was *really* good. He *knew* what he was doing."[296]

Jan admitted that she was drawn to "the older guys because they had this great Hollywood history." Gene didn't hold back when recalling how mean Sonja Henie was, and how difficult Gloria Grahame was to deal with while filming *Oklahoma!* When I asked Jan about Maureen Reagan, she reflected, "He talked about her often … really seemed to have warm thoughts about her. Being an interviewer, I tried getting more info but to no avail. But he did mention that he didn't feel he could be enough for the family to join it."[297] Jan and Gene would reconnect several years later after they both relocated to San Francisco.

In the Fall of 1978, after a year-long hiatus, Gene got back in the swing of directing. He opted for TV's *Quincy* starring Jack Klugman. *A Night to Raise the Dead* was an eerie, thought-provoking foray into political corruption during a typhoid epidemic. Several other series and genres would occupy Gene until his final television directorial credits in the Fall of 1979. For *Fantasy Island,* he directed a segment titled, (ironically) "The Dancer," in which a ballerina (Carol Lynley) tries to get back in shape after eight years of not performing. Happiness depends on rejuvenating the "butterfly" within. Familiar territory for Gene Nelson. Gene also reunited with his co-star from *Oklahoma!* – Shirley Jones. He directed the second segment of her series, *Shirley.* Like *The Partridge Family*, the story focused on the challenges of an attractive widowed mother.

Gene attempted to lure former co-star Doris Day back to the big screen. He reflected afterwards, "I saw Doris a couple of months before she moved up to Carmel. I went over to her house in Beverly

Hills. I had an idea for a script for her to do with Rock [Hudson]. It was a little difficult to talk, because her twenty-five dogs were always in the way."[298] Gene could see that Doris' mind no longer focused on Hollywood. She was focused solely on relocating to Carmel, and her promotion of the Doris Day Pet Foundation.

***S.O.B.*** **(1981) with Julie Andrews (Paramount)**

In the Spring of 1980, actor Gene Nelson headed to Malibu to make his cinema swansong. Producer/Director Blake Edwards' $12 million satire, *S.O.B.*, must have sounded promising. The cast included Julie Andrews, William Holden, Robert Preston, Shelley Winters, Richard Mulligan and Gene's "old pal" Larry Hagman. In this spoof of Hollywood, Mulligan's character, a successful producer, is beside himself after making his first flop. His hilarious attempts at suicide are the focus of the plot (also written by Blake Edwards). Mulligan is inspired to re-edit the film into a porn musical starring his wife (Andrews). Critics were sharply divided as to the results. Gene Nelson, assigned the miniscule role of a business manager named Clive, is seen briefly in two scenes, mumbling one line. The film flopped financially. After *S.O.B.* was released, Edwards (Gene's former chum from "The Mouse Pack") attempted to have his name removed from the writing credits.

Gene returned to *Fantasy Island* as an ex-vet in *Daddy's Little Girl* (1982). Three flying squadrons who were in the Philippines reunite to claim fatherhood of a young bride-to-be, after she finds out that her mother's husband is *not* her real dad. Her mother

(Carolyn Jones) is put on the defensive. It turns out that the *real* dad lost his life in the war while saving his comrades. The proceedings were a little racy, but touching.

Per the *Hollywood Reporter*, Gene joined Marge Champion for a two-week "That's Dancing" cruise from Florida to Southampton, England. This 1986 venture aboard the Royal Viking included lectures, film clips, and dance classes. Gene capped his acting career with a 1987 appearance on the Angela Lansbury detective series, *Murder, She Wrote. The Corpse Flew First Class* featured Gene, flying first class, harboring a dark secret.

**Murder She Wrote (1987) "The Corpse Flew First Class" Gene and Mary Jo Catlett**

<<>>

While attending Santa Monica College, son Douglas Nelson was cast in the film sex-comedy *The Last American Virgin* (1982). After playing this "uncredited" role, Doug opted to study acting professionally. He studied dramatic arts at the Sal Dano Workshop in Los Angeles. Victoria Nelson was still in high school. Their father took a rather unexpected step himself in the field of education. In the Fall of 1989, Gene Nelson earned the honor of becoming …

## Professor of Theatre Arts

San Francisco State University. Founded in 1899, the 141-acre campus near the Pacific Coast, had its own atmosphere—apart from the proverbial "City by the Bay." In the 1960's, SF State gained a reputation for drawing students who were liberal-leaning and anti-establishment. While I was there (majoring in Sociology), I became involved with the Vietnam Day Committee, a coalition of political and student groups, who distributed information about war-profiteering and the issues surrounding our involvement in Vietnam. We also had the first Black Student Union, and students supporting the Gay Liberation Front. Yes, there were lots of protests, rallies, class closures, all while trying to study for final exams. Keeping calm amid the chaos was a skill worth developing. It was a stimulating atmosphere, to say the least.

With a minor in Drama, I especially enjoyed directing scenes from film classics such as *Dinner at Eight*. Twenty-years later, students were fortunate to enroll in drama classes conducted by a true veteran: Gene Nelson—Professor of Theatre Arts. Gene welcomed the opportunity, and enjoyed himself. He commented during an interview with Skip E. Lowe,

> *I'm teaching at SF State. Theatre Arts. Acting, directing – all that stuff. And, I love it! The course that I teach is called "The Complete Actor-Director." I teach two-hour sessions. I usually start it out with a little movement - getting them up - getting their bodies moving. Actors have to be able to move. You know what I mean? Body language. They have to know where the muscles are and how to control them. Then we start doing physical mimes. Then we do the same mime in slow motion. I love the first time I give the exercise to the class, because they really don't feel the weight of that until they start to do it. They are absolutely surprised.*[299]

Aside from being an instructor, Gene directed and choreographed the school's largest production, the musical *Twain!* With a budget of $18,000, a cast of thirty brought to life a tribute to the legendary Mark Twain. During Gene's interview with Skip Lowe, Lowe commented, "You look very happy. Very content." Gene laughed. "It must be from living in San Francisco. I'm not bad for a 70-year-old man, huh?" Lowe then asked Gene how many times he had been married. Gene braced himself a bit, and firmly held up two fingers. He gave no indication, that a *third* matrimonial trip was near at hand.

While at San Francisco State, Gene's teaching reached across the globe upon the release of his video "Come Tap With Me." Filmed at The Debbie Reynolds Studio in Los Angeles, Gene cheerfully instructs a dozen students, beginning with the basics of "shuffling," then on to a full routine with turns, slides and leans. In April 1989, Gene invited his friend Jan Wahl, now a Bay Area entertainment reporter, to accompany him to the Academy Awards. Wahl, an alumnus of San Francisco State, told the press, "I felt like I was in Oz," admitting she wished more old-time movie stars were in attendance.[300] Wahl was grateful for her reunion with Gene Nelson. She explained to me,

> *He came back into my life. We became very close. And, I knew he was hurting. He was a haunted kind of guy. He wanted to be bigger. Gene told me everything. He was really forthcoming. Gene Nelson was so out there about telling you stuff. You know the big scandal about him and Jane Powell? Well, that apparently hurt him tremendously in Hollywood. There was a bitterness that Gene kept toward the business. He never got as far as his talent should have taken him. He wasn't the star he should have been.[301]*

**Jan Wahl (April 1989) (photo by Privette)** *Sausalito Marin Scope*

In spite of being "a haunted kind of guy," unlike many celebrities, Gene Nelson managed to move on … and make a difference. Tap dancer/historian Rusty Frank fondly recalled Gene telling her and other dancers, "Onward, upward, and don't look back."[302] Obviously, it was advice that he was telling himself.

<<>>

After his second semester at SF State, Gene headed for a "class reunion" at Warner Bros. The official re-dedication of the studio was held June 2, 1990, and was filmed "live" as the documentary: *Warner Bros.-Celebration of Tradition.* Attended by more than 150 stars, alumni in attendance went all the way back to Ruby Keeler. Co-stars of Gene, Virginia Mayo and Ronald Reagan also joined in the festivity. Mayo would retain a soft spot for Gene long after he passed away. Warner Bros. historian Kevin Wedman recalled, "I had the pleasure of meeting Virginia. I was surprised at her vulnerability when I mentioned Gene Nelson. A tear came to her eye. She missed him."[303] Not long after the Warner Bros. celebration, Gene Nelson received his star on the legendary Hollywood Walk of Fame—7005 Hollywood Blvd.

In July 1990, *The Hollywood Reporter* announced that Gene had wed Jean Martin. The couple were married at the Westlake home of Gene's friend Pat Horn. Horn had also hosted the ceremony for Gene and ex-wife Marilyn. No details as to Jean Martin's backstory were provided. The article simply stated that the couple resided near his work at San Francisco State. Home for Gene and Jean, was actually the scenic town of Atherton, about thirty miles south of the campus. When I talked with Jan Wahl in 2023, she shed a good deal of light on the subject.

> *I introduced Gene to Jean. I knew her. She was a socialite from the Peninsula. By that time, Gene was in need of emotional counseling and financial support. I introduced them to each other, and I'm very glad I did, because he made her happy and she made him happier than he was. Jean was accommodating. It was her money. Gene didn't save his money very well. He was sad and disillusioned about his own affairs.*

Wahl added that "socialite" Jean was also using Gene Nelson for his celebrity. For years she was involved with Bay Area dance and art festivals. A choreographer herself, Jean had worked with Charles Pierce, one of the foremost female impersonators.[304] Wahl concluded her commentary regarding Jean Martin by saying, "She cut me off, because Gene was my former boyfriend."

**Charles Pierce, Gene, Jean Martin (c.1991-92)**

While in Atherton, Gene commuted to the town of Saratoga, where he directed and choreographed *Stepping Out*. The musical comedy had heart, as it detailed a group of amateur tap-dancers in North London, who practice at a dingy church hall, until they gain notoriety after doing a charity show. Former director C. Michael Traw recalled in 2023, "Gene became my friend when he came to see our production of *Follies*, and came back to direct *Stepping Out*. He was so supportive of our South Bay Musical Theater. So glad to have known him."[305] Most likely, this was Gene Nelson's final gig as director. Gene and Jean parted ways in 1994. Again, no news coverage as to the particulars of their divorce. Gene returned to Los Angeles, where he resided in Sherman Oaks.

Miriam Nelson recalled that upon returning from sightseeing Australia and New Zealand in 1996, she received a call from son Chris. Chris informed her that Gene "was ill and in a coma."[306] In her autobiography, Miriam noted that she and Chris went to the Motion Picture Country Home. "We visited Gene," she recalled, "… we were all there when he died." Gene passed away on September 16. Daughter Victoria Gordo, who was living in New York City, informed the press that her father had been suffering from cancer. Gene was seventy-six.

The Motion Picture Country Home in Woodland Hills was founded in 1940. The nature-laden retirement community in the San Fernando Valley, provided lodging and health care for retired film folk. Over the years, the Country Home became refuge for numerous classic film stars. Ability to pay was not an issue. It was Hollywood taking care of its own. Following cremation, Gene's ashes were taken to the historic pier in Santa Monica, where they were scattered into the Pacific Ocean. He was survived by his three children and three grandchildren. Gene's mother, Lenore, had died in Los Angeles a couple of months before her son, on July 3. Lenore was ninety-eight. Son Chris encouraged his mother to create a memorial service for his father, which she did. The memorial included a catered lunch. "I think Gene would have been pleased," wrote Miriam.

In 2015, daughter Victoria reflected:

> *My father was a great talent, always getting left out of what he deserved when it came to recognition. I know his life and relationships weren't always easy, but his talent and artwork spoke for itself. Besides being a Hollywood great, he was my dad. Not perfect, not always there, but always giving of himself to new talent 100%. I love him, and miss him.*[307]

Gene Nelson's innate ability for transition and redefining himself, enabled him to assist *others*. Not that he didn't entertain disappointment. He admitted to having a "fair share of regrets" regarding his career choices.[308] While appearing in *Follies*, he told a reporter, "Sure, I've been tempted to take the defeatist attitude and say, 'the hell with it.'"[309] Despite such "temptation," the world of entertainment benefited from his ingenuity, his ability of "being there" … a reflection, not so much of his celebrity, but of his presence. The healing balm of humor also propelled him forward. Gene summed up his own success in 1989, recalling the logo on a red T-shirt that someone had gifted him. "I think it sums up my whole creative philosophy," he mused. The logo?

*I didn't know it was impossible when I did it* [310]

# Afterword

**Chris (2014)**   **Douglas (2020)**   **Victoria (2017)**

The progeny of Eugene Leander Berg gravitated toward steady careers. Son Christopher, has focused on his career as a television editor. His legacy includes such series as *China Beach* and *Bates Motel*, with occasional directing assignments (*Lazarus Man*). Chris has been nominated several times for a Prime Time Emmy, winning for the series *Lost* (2004). During recent years, sharing knowledge and experience has become Chris' passion. Chris provided his father with three grandsons: Chris Jr., Matthew, and Josh, and a great-granddaughter Emma.

Son Douglas Morgan Nelson acted in films and several TV series, including *General Hospital*. After studying photography at Brooks Institute, he focused on being a headshot photographer for actors. The results were presented to agents and casting directors. Douglas fostered the philosophy, "The Eyes are the Windows of the Soul." It was his main profession for over thirty-five years. In early February 2023, I sent Douglas a message asking for input for his father's biography. When I didn't hear back after several weeks, I learned that Douglas passed away peacefully, at his home, on February 19, 2023. He was 60 years old.

Daughter Victoria Leandra Nelson Gordo, after pursuing a career in graphic design, is currently a realtor in the Fort Lauderdale area of Florida. Her mother Marilyn was also a realtor. Victoria has two children, Veronica and Victor.

<<>>

Miriam Nelson wrote a memoir, *My Life Dancing with the Stars* (2009). Upon its release, she attended a book-signing at Cinecon 45 in Hollywood (September 2009). Miriam and I had the same publisher (BearManor). Not knowing the backstory of her and ex-husband Gene's relationship, I was hesitant to ask her about him. A missed opportunity, to say the least. When I began my Gene Nelson research a decade later, Miriam's book was a godsend. Miriam passed away at her home in Beverly Hills, on August 12, 2018. Son Chris, was at her side. Miriam was 98. *The Hollywood Reporter* indicated, "When asked if she would ever retire, she replied, 'Not as long as the phone keeps ringing.' She was tap dancing a week before her death."[311]

**Miriam Nelson was a guest author at Cinecon 2009 in Hollywood (Photo by Joel Bellagio)**

<<>>

London-based writer and film aficionado Graceann Macleod, offered her keen eye and talent to proofread the Gene Nelson biography. I couldn't have done it without her. This is our seventh venture together. She and her husband David, are especially devoted to all-things-Buster-Keaton. Our mutual friend Jenny Paxson, who worked on behalf of film preservation for the Library of Congress Packard Campus, kept an eye out for all-things-Gene-Nelson. Jenny and her husband Larry Smith have been generous providing material from their own private collection of film memorabilia. Their invitations for me to introduce films at the Packard Campus, starring actors I have written about, is truly appreciated.

As always, the prolific author James Robert Parish was a guiding light with suggestions and insight. "I think a lot of people, like me, will be surprised by the scope/depth of Gene Nelson's career and life per your upcoming book," he encouraged.[312] Parish has written numerous (and indispensable) film biographies/reference books. My research for Gene Nelson was abetted by Parish's books: *The Fox Girls* (1971) and *Hollywood Songsters: Volume 2* (2003). Check out Jim's impressive resume at: (www.jamesrobertparish.com/books. html). Two other invaluable sources covering Gene's legacy were Tony Thomas' *That's Dancing!* (1984 - Abrams Press), and Rusty E. Frank's *Tap!* (1990 - Da Capo Press). Both authors had full cooperation of Gene Nelson. Rusty, who met Gene in 1988, tap danced with Gene and some friends for several months. Just for the fun of it! Thanks to Rusty, in June 1989, Gene penned some valuable details about his youth, his tour in *This is the Army*, and his early foray into making films.

Author Stephen Michael Shearer whose acclaimed *Gloria Swanson – The Ultimate Star* (2013) was essential for my *Herbert Marshall – A Biography* (2018), facilitated my contact with Gary Conway. Actor/artist/winemaker Conway, now living in San Luis Obispo, worked with Gene Nelson in three episodes of the popular series *Burke's Law* (1963-64). My December 2022 conversation with Conway was most helpful. He commented that acting is a "team effort"—noting that his director and co-star Gene Nelson, felt the same way.

**San Francisco - KRON Morning News – Scott interviewed by Jan Wahl (August 9, 2008)**

As my research and writing came to closure, I had the good fortune to come across a 1989 San Francisco news article about Bay Area radio/TV personality and reporter, Jan Wahl. In said article, Wahl mentioned that she had gone to the Academy Awards with "her actor/director friend, Gene Nelson." I immediately sent Wahl a message, to which she enthusiastically replied. Her heartfelt sharing of her friendship/love relationship with Gene, gave texture and soul to the final chapter. What Jan shared allows admirers to step into Gene Nelson's shoes, and sense the emotions and challenges he faced while choreographing his ... final transition.

<<>>


Connecticut, Nantucket, Washington D.C., Virginia, Florida, Arizona, Palm Springs, Hollywood, San Francisco, Berkeley .... over the last two decades, my husband Joel and I have enjoyed many adventures while doing research and visiting friends and family of the screen icons I have written about. Joel Bellagio's input has been invaluable, and he has kept me in good humor. Humor and heart provided an atmosphere of clarity and insight, as I moved forward into the lives of people I never had the pleasure of meeting, except on screen. Joel has created an informative and visually captivating website on my behalf: (www.scottobrienauthor.com)

**Tucson (2005) Scott and Joel visit friends of Kay Francis (Photo by Kay's friend Lou Ames) 2.25X2 inches**

Publisher Ben Ohmart (BearManor Media) has a legacy of championing the stories of "forgotten" stars. Since I submitted my first manuscript in 2004, Ben has been on board for all nine of my biographies. Ben's support has been a definite factor in my contemplating the question, "Who's next?" The BearManor catalogue includes, as their website indicates, "over 900 outstanding subjects from the obscure to the eminent." (www.bearmanormedia. com)

# Credits

***Foolin' Ourselves*** (closed while on tour – Tucson, Phoenix, Santa Barbara); By William Barnes and Robert Rodgers; Producer: Paul Gregory; Cast: Gene Nelson (Mr. Magic), Sue Carson, Joyce Jameson, Paul Jayson

**1957**

***Darling, I'm Yours*** (Curran Theatre, San Francisco) May 1957; Comedy by Fred and Elaine Shevin; Director: Jess Kimmel; Cast: Gene Nelson (Mike Sawyer), Lisa Gaye, Anne Gwynne, Philip Reed

**1958**

***Oklahoma*** (Center Theatre, New York) (15 performances) By Richard Rodgers and Oscar Hammerstein; Cast: Gene Nelson (Will Parker), Helen Gallagher, Betty Garde, Harvey Lembeck, Herbert Banke, Owen Martin, Lois O'Brien

(Denver-July 7-21) Cast: Gene Nelson, Helen Gallagher, Betty Garde

**1960**

***Hit the Deck*** (Jones Beach Marine Theatre, Long Island) (June 23-September 11) by Vincent Youmans; Producer: Guy Lombardo; D: Edward Greenberg, Cast: Gene Nelson (Bilge Smith), Jane Kean, Betty Ann Grove, Jules Munshin

**1971-1972**

***Follies*** (Colonial Theatre, Boston) (Preview: February 24-March 20, 1971) Book: James Goldman; Producer/Director: Harold Prince & Michael Bennett; Music/Lyrics: Stephen Sondheim; Cast: Alexis Smith, Gene Nelson (Buddy), Dorothy Collins, Yvonne DeCarlo, John McMartin, Fifi D'Orsay, Ethel Shutta, Michael Misita, Graciela Daniele, Mary Jane Houdina, Dick LaTessa, Fred Kelly

***Follies*** (Winter Garden Theatre, New York) (April 4, 1971-July 1, 1972)

***Follies*** (Muny Theatre, St. Louis) (July 3-9, 1972)

***Follies*** (Shubert Theatre, Los Angeles) (July 22-October 1, 1972)

**1974**

***Music, Music*** (City Center 55th Street Theatre, New York) (April 9, 1974-May 12, 1974) Musical Revue; Director: Martin Charnin; Footnotes: Alan Jay Lerner; Choreography: Tony Stevens; Cast: Gene Nelson, Larry Kent, Karen Morrow, Donna McKechnie, Robert Guillaume, Gail Nelson

**1974-75**

***Good News*** (St. James Theatre, New York) (Dec. 16, 1974-Jan. 4, 1975) Producer: Harry Rigby; Director: Abe Burrows; Music: Ray Henderson, B.G. DeSylva, Lew Brown; Cast: Alice Faye, Gene Nelson (Bill Johnson), Stubby Kaye

**1983**

***Star Time*** (Pantages Theatre, Hollywood) (January 1983) Music & Comedy revue; Director/Choreographer: Gene Nelson; Cast: Edie Adams, Vivian Blane, Peter Lind Hayes, Frankie Laine, Hildegarde, Allan Jones, Gene Bell

***A Period of Adjustment*** (Summer of 1983) Gene directed a Hollywood stage production of Tennessee Williams' light-hearted story

**1989**

***Twain*** (San Francisco State University) (November 30-December 9, 1990) Musical by John Everest; Director/Choreographer: Gene Nelson

**1993**

***Stepping Out*** (South Bay Musical Theatre, Saratoga) (January-February 6, 1993); Comedy by Richard Harris; Music by: Denis King and Mary Stewart-David; Director/Choreographer: Gene Nelson; Cast: C. Michael Traw, et. al.


**SCREEN - Actor**

**1939**

***Second Fiddle*** 20th Century-Fox D: Sidney Lanfield; Cast: Sonja Henie, Tyrone Power, Rudy Vallee, Edna Mae Oliver, Mary Healy, Lyle Talbot, Alan Dinehart, Minna Gombell, Spencer Charters, Gene Berg (dancer-skater)

***Everything Happens at Night*** 20th Century-Fox D: Irving Cummings; Cast: Sonja Henie, Ray Milland, Robert Cummings, Maurice Moscovitch, Leonid Kinskey, Alan Dinehart, Gene Berg (skater – scenes deleted)

**1943**

***This is the Army*** Warner Bros. (Based on Irving Berlin musical) D: Michael Curtiz; Cast: George Murphy, Joan Leslie, Ronald Reagan, George Tobias, Alan Hale Sr., George Butterworth, Dolores Costello, Una Merkel, Rosemary DeCamp, Bess Flowers, James MacColl, Gene Berg (Soldier – uncredited), Dan Dailey (Soldier – uncredited); Guest stars: Irving Berlin, Kate Smith, Joe Louis

**1947**

***I Wonder Who's Kissing Her Now*** 20th Century-Fox D: Lloyd Bacon; Cast: June Haver, Mark Stevens, Martha Stewart, Reginald Gardner, Lenore Aubert, William Frawley, Gene Nelson (Tommy Yale)

**1948**

***Gentleman's Agreement*** 20th Century-Fox D: Elia Kazan; Cast: Gregory Peck, Dorothy McGuire, John Garfield, Celeste Holm, Anne Revere, June Havoc, Albert Dekker, Jane Wyatt, Dean Stockwell. Gene Nelson (G.I.)

***The Walls of Jericho*** 20th Century-Fox D: John M. Stahl; Cast: Cornell Wilde, Linda Darnell, Anne Baxter, Kirk Douglas, Ann Dvorak, Marjorie Rambeau, Gene Nelson (assistant prosecutor)

***Apartment for Peggy*** 20th Century-Fox D: George Seaton; Cast: Jeanne Crain, William Holden, Edmund Gwenn, Gene Lockhart, Gene Nelson (Jerry)

**1950**

***The Daughter of Rosie O'Grady*** Warner Bros. D: David Butler; Cast: June Haver, Gordon MacRae, James Barton, S.Z. Sakall, Gene Nelson (Doug Martin), Debbie Reynolds, Marcia Mae Jones, Jane Darwell

***Tea for Two*** Warner Bros. D: David Butler; Cast: Doris Day, Gordon MacRae, Gene Nelson (Tommy Trainor), Patrice Wymore, Eve Arden, Billy De Wolfe, S.Z. Sakall, Virginia Gibson, Bess Flowers

***The West Point Story*** Warner Bros. D: Roy Del Ruth; Cast: James Cagney, Virginia Mayo, Doris Day, Gordon MacRae, Gene Nelson (Hal Courtland)

## 1951

***Lullaby of Broadway*** Warner Bros. D: David Butler; Cast: Doris Day, Gene Nelson (Tom Farnham), S.Z. Sakall, Billy De Wolfe, Gladys George, Florence Bates, Page Cavanaugh Trio, Bess Flowers

***Painting the Clouds with Sunshine*** Warner Bros. D: David Butler; Cast: Dennis Morgan, Virginia Mayo, Gene Nelson (Ted Lansing), Lucille Norman, S. Z. Sakall, Virginia Gibson, Tom Conway, Wallace Ford, Bess Flowers

***Starlift*** Warner Bros. D: Roy Del Ruth; Cast: Doris Day, Gordon MacRae, Virginia Mayo, Gene Nelson (himself), Ruth Roman, James Cagney, Gary Cooper, Virginia Gibson, Phil Harris, Frank Lovejoy, Lucille Norman, Louella Parsons, Randolph Scott, Jane Wyman, Patrice Wymore, Janice Rule, Jack Larson

## 1952

***She's Working Her Way Through College*** Warner Bros. D: H. Bruce Humberstone; Cast: Virginia Mayo, Ronald Reagan, Gene Nelson (Don Weston), Don DeFore, Phyllis Thaxter, Patrice Wymore, Roland Winters, Bess Flowers

## 1953

***She's Back on Broadway*** Warner Bros. D: Gordon Douglas; Cast: Virginia Mayo, Gene Nelson (Gordon Evans), Frank Lovejoy, Steve Cochran, Patrice Wymore, Virginia Gibson

***Three Sailors and a Girl*** Warner Bros. D: Roy Del Ruth; Cast: Jane Powell, Gordon MacRae, Gene Nelson (Twitch), Sam Levene, George Givot, Veda Ann Borg, Burt Lancaster, Merv Griffin, Jack Larson, Bess Flowers

## 1954

***Crime Wave*** Warner Bros. D: Andre DeToth; Cast: Sterling Hayden, Gene Nelson (Steve Lacey), Phyllis Kirk, Ted de Corsia, Charles Bronson

***So This is Paris*** Universal-International D: Richard Quine; Cast: Tony Curtis, Gloria DeHaven, Gene Nelson (Al Howard), Corinne Calvert, Paul Gilbert

**1955**

***Oklahoma!*** RKO Musical by: Rogers & Hammerstein D: Fred Zinnemann; Cast: Gordon MacRae, Gloria Graham, Gene Nelson (Will Parker), Charlotte Greenwood, Shirley Jones, Eddie Albert, James Whitmore, Rod Steiger, Barbara Lawrence, J.C. Flippen

***The Atomic Man (Timeslip)*** Todon Productions D: Ken Hughes; Cast: Gene Nelson (Mike Delaney), Faith Domergue, Joseph Tomelty, Leonard Williams, Barry MacKay, Peter Arne

***The Way Out (Dial 999)*** Todon Productions D: Montgomery Tully; Cast: Gene Nelson (Greg Carradine), Mona Freeman, John Bentley, Michael Goodliffe

**1961**

***20,000 Eyes*** API D: Jack Leewood; Cast: Gene Nelson (Dan Warren), Merry Anders, James Brown, John Banner, Rex Holman

***The Purple Hills*** API D: Maury Dexter; Cast: Gene Nelson (Gil Shepard), Joanna Barnes, Kent Taylor, Danny Zapien, Jerry Summers, Russ Bender

**1963**

***Thunder Island*** API D: Jack Leewood; Screenplay: Jack Nicholson and Don Devlin; Cast: Gene Nelson (Billy Poole), Fay Spain, Brian Kelly, Miriam Colon

**1981**

***S.O.B.*** Paramount D: Blake Edwards; Cast: Julie Andrews, William Holden, Marisa Berenson, Larry Hagman, Robert Loggia, Stuart Margolin, Richard Mulligan, Robert Preston, Craig Stevens,

Loretta Swit, Robert Vaughn, Robert Webber, Shelley Winters, Larry Storch, Gene Nelson (Clive Lytell)


**SCREEN – Director**

**1962**

***Hand of Death*** API D: Gene Nelson; Cast: John Agar, Paula Raymond, Stephen Dunne, Roy Gordon, John A. Alonzo, Jack Younger, Joe Besser

**1963**

***Hootenanny Hoot*** MGM D: Gene Nelson; Guest stars: Johnny Cash, Sheb Wooley, Brothers Four, Judy Henske, Joe & Eddie, George Hamilton IV, Chris Crosby, Gateway Trio; Cast: Peter Breck, Ruta Lee, Joby Baker, Pamela Austin, Maureen Reagan

**1964**

***Kissin' Cousins*** MGM D: Gene Nelson; Cast: Elvis Presley, Arthur O'Connell, Glenda Farrell, Jack Albertson, Pamela Austin, Cynthia Pepper, Yvonne Craig, Donald Woods, Tommy Farrell, Teri Garr, Maureen Reagan

***Your Cheatin' Heart*** MGM D: Gene Nelson; Cast: George Hamilton, Susan Oliver, Red Buttons, Arthur O'Connell, Shary Marshall, Rex Ingram

**1965**

***Harum Scarum*** MGM D: Gene Nelson; Cast: Elvis Presley, Mary Ann Mobley, Fran Jeffries, Michael Ansara, Jay Novello, Phillip Reed, Billy Barty

**1967**

***The Cool Ones*** Warner Bros. D: Gene Nelson; Cast: Roddy McDowall, Debbie Watson, Gil Peterson, Phil Harris, Robert Coote, Nita Talbot, George Furth, Mrs. Miller, Glen Campbell, Teri Garr, Ilona Massey


**TV**

**1948-1974 – Guest Star**

Gene Nelson appeared as guest star on numerous shows, including:

***The Ed Sullivan Show*** (January 1949) GN, Lon McCallister, Doretta Morrow, Forrest Tucker, Jule Styne, Sammy Cahn (August 1953) GN, Frankie Laine, Jimmy Boyd, Mitch Miller

***Your Show of Shows*** (May 1953) Sid Caesar, Imogene Coca, Carl Reiner, GN

***The Bob Hope Show*** (December 1953) Bob Hope, GN, Charles Farrell, Gale Storm, Pat Horn

***The Colgate Comedy Hour*** (November 1953) GN, Peggy Lee, Bud Abbott, Lou Costello, Dean Martin, Jerry Lewis, Pat Horn

(January 1954) GN, Ethel Merman, Jimmy Durante

(November 1954) GN, Bert Lahr, Vivian Blaine, Betty Furness (October 1955) cast members of the film *Oklahoma!*

***The Stork Club*** (January 1955) GN, Charles Coburn, Edie Adams

***Shower of Stars*** (June 1955) Betty Grable, GN, Shirley MacLaine, Ethel Merman, Jack Oakie, Dan Dailey, Harry James, Red Skelton, Patricia Rosemond

***The Patti Page Show*** (November 1955) Perry Como, GN, Ray Charles singers

***Stage Show*** (November 1955) GN, Eddy Arnold, Dorsey Brothers

***The Rosemary Clooney Show*** (May 1956) GN

***The Dinah Shore Show*** (August 1956) GN, Janet Blair, Fernando Lamas

***The Steve Allen Plymouth Show*** (November 1956) GN, Duke Ellington

***Juke Box Jury*** (December 1956) GN, Phyllis Kirk

***Modern Romances*** (March 1958) GN guest host

***The Garry Moore Show*** (March 1960) GN, Carol Burnett, Gertrude Berg

***You Bet Your Life*** (Groucho Marx) (March 1960) GN, Melinda Marx

***The Bell Telephone Hour*** (November 1959) GN, John Raitt (January 1960) GN, Louis Armstrong, Shirley Jones (February 1961) GN

(April 1962) GN, José Iturbi, Jo Stafford, Tommy Sands

***Dateline: Hollywood*** (June 1967) GN, Joanna Barnes, Rona Barrett, Elvis Presley

***The David Frost Show*** (June 1971) GN, Alexis Smith, Yvonne De Carlo, Dorothy Collins, Stephen Sondheim

***The Mike Douglas Show*** (May 1971) GN, Ray Bolger
(April 1972) GN, Carol Channing

***The Tonight Show*** (May 1971) GN, James Coco
(August 1972) GN, Joey Bishop, Cleveland Amory

***The Merv Griffin Show*** (July 1972) GN, Alexis Smith, Yvonne De Carlo, Dorothy Collins, Stephen Sondheim, Harold Prince
(August 1972) GN, Ann Miller, Sandra Dee, Ritz Brothers

***Grammy Salutes Oscar*** (March 1974) Gene Kelly (host), GN, Ann Miller, Janet Blair, Gordon MacRae, Tony Martin, Frankie Avalon, Rosemary Clooney, Henry Mancini, Cyd Charisse, Dennis Morgan, Jane Withers

## 1954-1987 - Actor

***Shower of Stars*** (October 1954) *Lend an Ear*; GN, Sheree North, Edgar Bergen, Mario Lanza

***Studio One*** (January 1955) *The Missing Men*; GN, Edward Andrews, Jack Klugman

***The Best of Broadway*** (May 1955) *Broadway*; GN, Piper Laurie, Joseph Cotten

***General Electric Theatre*** (October 1955) *Tryout*; GN, Ann Harding

***Ford Television Theatre*** (December 1955) *A Kiss for Santa*; GN, Kathryn Grant, Virginia Field

***Celebrity Playhouse*** (February 1956) *Tantrum Size 12*; GN, Kathryn Grant, Charles Herbert

***Climax!*** (February 1956) *Nightmare by Day*; GN, Mary Astor, Colleen Gray, Katy Jurado

***Matinee Theatre*** (April 1956) *Fiddlin' Man*; GN, Murvyn Vye

***Chevron Hall of Stars*** (April 1956), *Yesterday's Mice*; GN, Helen Westcott

***Stage 7*** (September 1956) *Yesterday's Mice* (different cast); GN, Barbara Eiler

***Schlitz Playhouse*** (September 1956) *Moment of Vengeance*; GN, Ward Bond, Angie Dickinson

***Kaiser Aluminum Hour*** (April 1957) *A Man's Game*; GN, Nanette Fabray

***Maverick*** (February 1958) *Trail West to Fury*; GN, James Garner, Jack Kelly, Efrem Zimbalist Jr.

***Kraft Theatre*** (February 1958) *The Woman at High Hollow*; GN, Susan Oliver, Skip Homeier, Estelle Winwood

***Northwest Passage*** (January 1959) *The Fourth Brother*; GN, Buddy Ebsen, Lee Van Cleef, Grant Withers

***Have Gun – Will Travel*** (February 1959) *The Return of the Lady*; GN, Richard Boone, Patricia Medina

***The Millionaire*** (March 1959) *Millionaire Marcia Forrest*; GN, Marvin Miller, Nancy Gates

***Bat Masterson*** (April 1959) *Brunette Bombshell*; GN, Gene Barry, Rebecca Welles

***Oh! Susannah*** (October 1959) *One, Two, Ski!*; GN, Gale Storm, ZaSu Pitts

***Rawhide*** (October 1959) *Incident of the Shambling Man*; GN, Anne Francis, Victor McLaglen, Eric Fleming, Clint Eastwood

***Alcoa Theatre*** (October 1959) *Tom, Dick, and Harry*; GN, Irene Ryan

***Philip Marlow*** (March 1960) *Murder is a Grave Affair*; GN, Philip Carey

***Black Saddle*** (April 1960) *The Cabin*; GN, Lee Van Cleef

***Law of the Plainsman*** (May 1960) *Trojan Horse*; GN, Michael Ansara

***Men into Space*** (May 1960) *Beyond the Stars*; GN, William Lundigan

***Gunsmoke*** (June 1959) *Blue Horse*; GN, James Arness, Dennis Weaver

(October 1959) *Saludos*; GN, James Arness, Amanda Blake

(October 1960) *Say Uncle*; GN, James Arness, Milburn Stone

***Hallmark Hall of Fame*** (October 1960) *Shangri-La*; GN (Actor/ Choreographer), Richard Basehart, Marisa Pavan, Alice Ghostley, Helen Gallagher, Claude Rains

***The Detectives*** (May 1961) *Duty Date*; GN, Robert Taylor, Barbara Nichols

***Follow the Sun*** (March 1962) *Not Aunt Charlotte!*; GN, Tuesday Weld, Laraine Day, Barry Coe, Jane Kean, Gigi Perreau, Brett Halsey

***77 Sunset Strip*** (September 1963) *5* (Five episodes) (Directed by William Conrad); GN, Efrem Zimbalist Jr., Leonid Kinskey, Victor Buono, Wally Cox, Richard Conte, Burgess Meredith, William Shatner, Diane McBain, Clint Walker

***Burke's Law*** (October 1963) *Who Killed Harris Crown?*; GN, Gene Barry, Gary Conway, Regis Toomey, Joan Blondell, Barbara Eden, Eva Gabor, Ruth Roman, Juliet Prowse, Charles Lane

(September 1964) *Who Killed Vaudeville?*; GN, Gene Barry, Gary Conway, Gloria Swanson, Gypsy Rose Lee, Phil Harris

***Ironside*** (October 1967) *Tagged for Murder*; GN, Raymond Burr, Jack Kelly, Bruce Lee

***Mod Squad*** (November 1968) *Find Tara Chapman!* (Directed by Gene Nelson); GN, Michael Cole, Clarence Williams III, Peggy Lipton, Della Reese

***ITV Saturday Night Theatre*** (January 1970) *Married Alive*; GN, Diana Rigg, Robert Culp

***Family Flight*** (1972) (TV movie); GN, Rod Taylor, Dina Merrill

***Circle of Fear*** (January 1973) *Death's Head*; GN, Janet Leigh, Rory Calhoun

***A Brand New Life*** (1973) (TV movie); GN, Cloris Leachman, Martin Balsam, Mildred Dunnock, Wilfrid Hyde-White

***Fantasy Island*** (1982) *Daddy's Little Girl*; GN, Ricardo Montalban, Carolyn Jones, John Carradine, Alan Hale Jr., Genie Francis

***Murder She Wrote*** (January 1987) *The Corpse Flew First Class*; GN, Angela Lansbury, Robert Walker Jr., Mary Jo Catlett, David Hemmings

## 1958-1980 - Director

***Matinee Theatre*** (May 1958) *Prosper's Old Mother*; Mabel Albertson

***The Bell Telephone Hour*** (January 1960) *Our Musical Ambassadors*; Shirley Jones, Louis Armstrong, Jane Froman

***The Rifleman*** (1961-1962) (8 episodes); Chuck Connors, Johnny Crawford

***The Donna Reed Show*** (1962-1965) (22 episodes); Donna Reed, Carl Betz, Shelley Fabares, Paul Petersen; Guest Stars: Buster Keaton, Bess Flowers, Paul Winchell, Stuart Erwin, Bob Crane, Willie Mays, Ellen Corby

***Destry*** (1964) (4 episodes); John Gavin; Guest Stars: Fess Parker, Lee Van Cleef, Janet Blair, Ellen Corby

***The Farmer's Daughter*** (1963-1965) (7 episodes); Inger Stevens, William Windom, Cathleen Nesbitt; Guest Stars: Paul Lynde, Gloria Henry

***Vacation Playhouse*** (July 1964) *I and Claudie*; Ross Martin

***The Reporter*** (October 1964) *No Comment*; Robert Ryan, Gary Merrill, Harry Guardino

***Burke's Law*** (September 1964) *Who Killed Vaudeville?*; GN, Gene Barry, Gary Conway, Regis Toomey, Gloria Swanson, Gypsy Rose Lee, Phil Harris

(November 1964) *Who Killed the Richest Man in the World?*; Gene Barry, Gary Conway, Ricardo Montalban, George Hamilton, Smothers Brothers

***The Cara Williams Show*** (November 1964) *Get the Lead Out*; Cara Williams

***The Andy Griffith Show*** (November 1964) *Goodbye Sheriff Taylor*; Andy Griffith, Ron Howard, Don Knotts, Francis Bavier

(November 1964) *The Pageant*; Andy Griffith, Ron Howard, Don Knotts

***Gilligan's Island*** (March 1965) *The Return of Wrongway Feldman*; Bob Denver, Alan Hale Jr., Jim Backus, Tina Louise, Natalie Schafer, Hans Conried

***Tammy*** (October 1965) *The Poker Game*; Debbie Watson, Denver Pyle, Donald Woods, Ellen Corby

***I Dream of Jeannie*** (1965) (8 episodes); Barbara Eden, Larry Hagman, Bill Daily

***Where's Everett?*** (April 1966) (TV pilot); Alan Alda

***The Phyllis Diller Show*** (*The Pruitts of Southampton*) (September 1966) *Phyllis Goes Broke*; Phyllis Diller, Reginald Gardiner, Grady Sutton

***12 O'Clock High*** (January 1967) *A Long Time Dead*); Peter Graves, Paul Burke, Gil Peterson

***Laredo*** (February 1967) *Enemies and Brothers*; Neville Brand, Peter Brown

***Cowboy in Africa*** (October 1967) *Search for Survival*; Chuck Connors, Anne Baxter

***Iron Horse*** (1967) (3 episodes); Dale Robertson, Ellen Burstyn

***The Felony Squad*** (February 1967) *Echo of a Killing*; Howard Duff, Dennis Cole
  (October 1968) *Jury of One*; Howard Duff, Dennis Cole, Ben Alexander

***The F.B.I*** (1967-1970) (7 episodes); Efrem Zimbalist Jr.; Guest Stars: Burt Reynolds, Jimmy Lydon, Jeff Bridges

***Star Trek*** (January 1968) *The Gamesters of Triskelion*; William Shatner, Leonard Nimoy, DeForest Kelley

***Lancer*** (October 1968) *Blood Rock*; James Stacy, Andrew Duggan (December 1968) *Glory*; James Stacy, Andrew Duggan

***Blondie*** (1968-1969) (4 episodes); Will Hutchins, Patricia Harty, Jim Backus

***Mod Squad*** (1968-1971) (18 episodes); Michael Cole, Clarence Williams III, Peggy Lipton; Guest Stars: GN, Della Reese, Sammy Davis Jr., Lee Grant, Anita Louise, David Cassidy, Diane McBain, Barbara Rush, Danny Thomas

***Wake Me When the War is Over*** (1969) (TV movie); Ken Berry, Eva Gabor

***Hawaii 5-O*** (December 1969) *The Joker's Wild, Man, Wild!*; Jack Lord, James MacArthur, Peggy Ryan

***The Silent Force*** (September 1970) *Prosecutor*; Ed Nelson, Lynda Day George

(October 1970) *The Shopping List*; Ed Nelson, Percy Rodrigues, Dane Clark

***Dan August*** (October 1970) *The King is Dead*; Burt Reynolds, Norman Fell

(April 1971) *The Assassin*; Burt Reynolds, Norman Fell, Carolyn Jones

***The Most Deadly Game*** (January 1971) *The Lady from Praha*; George Maharis, Yvette Mimieux, Ralph Bellamy, Bert Convy

***The Letters*** (1973) (TV movie); Barbara Stanwyck, Jane Powell

***Ironside*** (November 1973) *Mind for Murder*; Raymond Burr, Don Galloway

***The Rookies*** (1973-1974) (5 episodes); Georg Stanford Brown, Kate Jackson

***Cannon*** (October 1973) *Target in the Mirror*; William Conrad, Claude Akins

(February 1974) *Where's Jennifer?*; William Conrad, Keye Luke

***Barnaby Jones*** (May 1974) *Dark Legacy*; Buddy Ebsen, Eileen Heckart

***Get Christie Love!*** (September 1974) *Market for Murder*; Teresa Graves

***Starsky and Hutch*** (September 1974) *Death Ride*; David Soul, Paul M. Glaser

***The Invisible Man*** (November 1975) *Stop When the Red Lights Flash*; David McCallum, Craig Stevens, Melinda O. Fee, Scott Brady

***McNaughton's Daughter*** (1976) (TV mini-series); Susan Clark, Ricardo Montalban, Gene Raymond, Vera Miles, Louise Latham, Ralph Bellamy

***San Pedro Beach Bums*** (October 1977) *Magnificent Moose*; Christopher Murney

(October 1977) *Winner's Circle*; Christopher Murney

***The American Girls*** (October 1978) *Little Girl Lost*; Karen Austin

***Quincy*** (December 1978) *A Night to Raise the Dead*); Jack Klugman

***Salvage 1*** (January 1979) *Dark Island)*; Andy Griffith, Richard Jaeckel

***The Bad News Bears*** (May 1979) *The Food Caper*; Jack Warden

***Operation Petticoat*** (June 1979) *Don't Drink the Shimbaka!*; Randolph Mantooth

(July 1979) *Matters of Honor*; Randolph Mantooth, Warren Berlinger

***Eischied*** (October 1979) *The Accused*; Joe Don Baker

***Shirley*** (November 1979) *Hard Hat*; Shirley Jones, Rosanna Arquette

***Fantasy Island*** (November 1979) *The Dancer/Nobody's There*; Ricardo Montalban, Herve Villechaize, Max Baer Jr., Carol Lynley, Michael Callen

***Dan August: The Jealousy Factor*** (1980) (TV movie that used archive footage from 1970) Co-Director with George McCowan; Burt Reynolds, Anne Francis, Norman Fell, Janice Rule

## 1959 - Choreographer

Gene Nelson was designated as choreographer for two TV series, in which he did not appear:

***The Eddie Fisher Show*** (January-February 1959)

***Some of Manie's Friends*** (March 3, 1959) Tribute to producer Manie Sacks. Cast: Perry Como, Dinah Shore, Frank Sinatra, Eddie Fisher, Rosemary Clooney, Kay Starr, Jane Wyman, Sid Caesar, Nat King Cole, Tony Martin, Bob Hope, Harry James, Danny Thomas

## 1990 - Video

***Come Tap with Me***

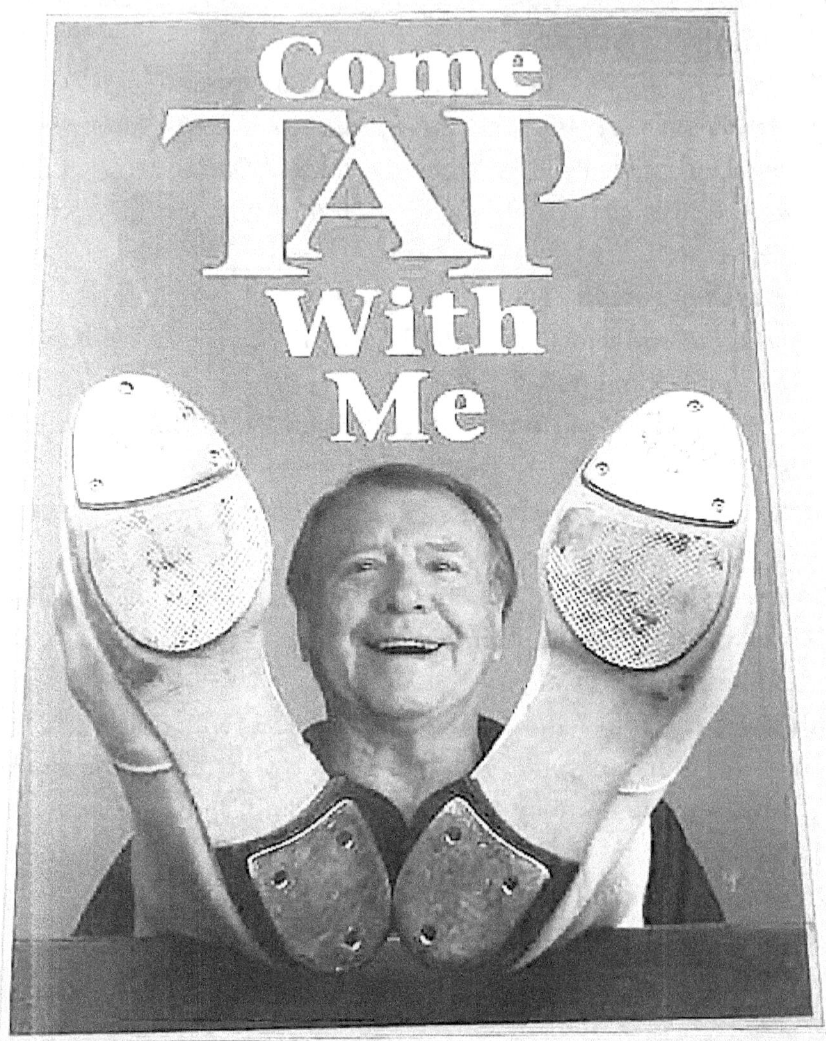
Come
TAP
With
Me

# **Photo Credits**

Photo Credits

Every effort has been made to trace the copyright holders of photographs in this book; if any have been inadvertently overlooked, the author and publisher will be pleased to make the necessary changes.

All MGM photos © Metro-Goldwyn-Mayer Studios Inc. All Rights Reserved

All Fox (20th Century-Fox) photos © 20th Century-Fox Film Corp. All Rights Reserved

All Warner Bros. photos © Warner Bros. Entertainment Inc. Co. All Rights Reserved

All Paramount photos © Paramount Pictures. All Rights Reserved

All Columbia photos Columbia Pictures-Sony Entertainment. All Rights Reserved

All Universal photos © Universal Studios. All Rights Reserved

All RKO photos © RKO Pictures LLC. All Rights Reserved

All Todon Productions photos © Todon Productions. All Rights Reserved

API Productions photos © API Productions. All Rights Reserved

All other photos, unless otherwise noted, are from the author's collection.

# About the Author

Scott O'Brien has paid tribute to eight deserving film legends, who had never had full-fledged biographies: Kay Francis, Virginia Bruce, Ann Harding, Ruth Chatterton, Sylvia Sidney, George Brent, Herbert Marshall and Elissa Landi. Scott has contributed numerous articles for publications such as *Films of the Golden Age*, *Classic Images*, and *Filmfax*. His guest appearances include the San Francisco Silent Film Festival, Cinecon 2009 in Hollywood, KRCB's *Outbeat Radio* and *A Novel Idea*, as well as Jan Wahl's "Inside Entertainment" for KRON-TV in San Francisco.

Scott introduced the film classics *Trouble in Paradise* (1932) and *Double Harness* (1933) at the Library of Congress's Packard Theater in Culpeper, Va. He has also appeared in two film documentaries: *Queer Icon – the Cult of Bette Davis* (2009) and *Reabhloidithe Hollywood* (2013) chronicling the career of George Brent, a former dispatcher for the IRA. Scott lives with his husband Joel Bellagio in Sonoma County. (website: www.scottobrienauthor.com)

# Endnotes


1    Tony Thomas, *That's Dancing!* Harry N. Abrams, Inc., c. 1984, p. 214

2    John A. Gallagher, Director/Actor Gene Nelson Talks Hollywood, (Interview – tvdays.com -Youtube) c. 1982

3    ibid.

4    Army Show Chorus 'Lovelies' Outdo the Real Article, *Evening Star* (DC), Oct. 3, 1942

5    Alan Anderson, The Songwriter Goes to War, Hal Leonard Corp., c. 2004, pg. 188

**Chapter One**

6    "Drove A Knife Into His Heart," *The Morning Astorian*, December 10, 1901

7    "Stabbed His Wife," *Morning Oregonian*, December 10, 1901

8    WWII Draft Registration for Gene Leander Berg (Serial Number: S-437) birthplace: Seattle; The 1920 Census (January 9) lists Leander and Lenore living on Willow Street in Seattle

9    Gene Nelson interview, Skip E. Lowe Looks at Hollywood, (weekly TV talk show, 1990)

10   "McKinley School", *Evening Outlook*, June 4, 1931

11   John A. Gallagher, Director/Actor Gene Nelson Talks Hollywood, (Interview – tvdays.com -Youtube) c.1982

12   Caroline Brooks, "He Wuz Mobbed!" Modern Screen, January 1953

13   John A. Gallagher, Director/Actor Gene Nelson Talks Hollywood, (Interview – tvdays.com -Youtube) c.1982

14   Tony Thomas, *That's Dancing!* Harry N. Abrams, Inc., c. 1984, pg. 214

15   Tony Thomas, *That's Dancing!*, Harry N. Abrams, Inc., c. 1984, pg. 214

16   Rusty E. Frank, *Tap!*, Da Capo Press, c.1994, pg. 191

17   Funeral Notices, *Evening Outlook*, May 22, 1934

18   Tony Thomas, *That's Dancing!*, Harry N. Abrams, Inc., c. 1984, pg. 214

19   Miriam Nelson, "How I Pursued My Husband," Photoplay, July 1951

20   Rusty E. Frank, *Tap!*, Da Capo Press, c. 1994, pg. 192

21   John A. Gallagher, Director/Actor Gene Nelson Talks Hollywood, (Interview – tvdays.com -Youtube) c.1982

22   Rusty E. Frank, *Tap!*, Da Capo Press, c. 1994, pg. 192

23   "School Hears Congressman," *Evening Outlook*, September 20, 1936

24   Rusty E. Frank, *Tap!*, Da Capo Press, c. 1994, pg. 192

25   "Samohi Student Officers," *Evening Outlook*, June 3, 1937

26   Rusty E. Frank, *Tap!* Da Capo Press, c. 1994, pg. 193

27   John A. Gallagher, Director/Actor Gene Nelson Talks Hollywood, (Interview – tvdays.com -Youtube) c.1982 Prival had performed ballet with the Metropolitan Opera, and was associated with ballet master Nico Charisse (first husband of Cyd Charisse)

**Chapter Two**

28   Lucie Neville, "Movie Monie – Stars Make It, Stooges Take It," *San Bernadino Sun*, August 25, 1940

29   John A. Gallagher, Director/Actor Gene Nelson Talks Hollywood, (Interview – tvdays.com -Youtube) c.1982

30   Rusty E. Frank, *Tap!*, Da Capo Press, c. 1994, pg. 193

31   Tony Thomas, *That's Dancing!* Abrams Press, c. 1984, pg. 217

32   James Robert Parish, *The Fox Girls*, Arlington House, c. 1971, pg. 274

33  "Sonja Henie-Fire on Ice", Biography (TV) interview with James Robert Parish, 1997

34  Richard Lockridge, review of *It Happens on Ice*, *The New York Sun*, October 11, 1940

35  Nikki Nichols, *Frozen in Time*, Clerisy Pr., c. 2008, pg. 81

36  Arthur Pollock, "It Happens on Ice is a Pretty Eyeful," *Brooklyn Eagle*, October 11, 1940

37  Jack Gaver, "Up and Down Broadway," *San Mateo Times*, April 24, 1941

38  "Ice Skaters Hold Out for Raise on Tour with Show," (UP) *Imperial Valley Press*, November 21, 1940

39  "Few in Ice Field Get Big Dough," *Billboard*, February 14, 1942

40  Tony Thomas, *That's Dancing!* Abrams Press, c. 1984, pg. 217

41  Miriam Nelson, *My Life Dancing With the Stars*, BearManor, c. 2009, pg. 48

42  "Emphasis on S.A. in Jukepix Made East," *Variety*, December 25, 1940

43  Miriam Nelson, *My Life Dancing With the Stars*, BearManor, c. 2009, pg. 53

44  "Miriam, in Audience, Went Up and Got Her Man," *P.M. Weekly*, November 30, 1941

45  Miriam Nelson, "I Married a Serviceman," *Photoplay*, February 1952

46  Rusty E. Frank, *Tap!*, Da Capo Press, c. 1994, pg. 193

47  Gene Nelson, "Our Christmas Love Story," *Modern Screen*, January 1952

48  Rusty E. Frank, *Tap!*, Da Capo Press, c. 1994, pg. 193

49  Tony Thomas, *That's Dancing!* Abrams Press, c. 1984, pg. 217

## Chapter Three

50  Gene Nelson, "Our Christmas Love Story," *Modern Screen*, January 1952

51   Miriam Nelson, "I Married a Serviceman," *Photoplay*, February 1952

52   Frances Ingram, "Gene Nelson – Athletic Grace," *Classic Images*, December 2005

53   Tony Thomas, *That's Dancing!* Abrams Press, c. 1984, pg. 219

54   Rusty E. Frank, *Tap!* Da Capo Press, c. 1994, pg. 194

55   Miriam Nelson, *My Life Dancing with the Stars*, BearManor, c. 2009, pg. 13

56   Cook Co., Illinois, U.S. Birth Certificate Index (Birthplace: Chicago; parents: Daniel Frankel and Miriam Bly)

57   Hal Eaton, "Going to Town," *Long Island Daily Press*, February 15, 1938

58   Miriam Nelson, *My Life Dancing with the Stars*, BearManor, c. 2009, pg. 29

59   Miriam Nelson interview, Skip E. Lowe Looks at Hollywood, (weekly TV talk show, 1998)

60   Miriam Nelson, *My Live Dancing with the Stars,* BearManor, c. 2009, pg. 31

61   Mark Barron, review of *Let's Play Fair*, *Times-Union*, January 30, 1938

62   Miriam Nelson, *My Life Dancing with the Stars*, BearManor, c. 2009, pg. 33

63   Rusty E. Frank, *Tap!* Da Capo Press, c. 1994, pg. 197

64   Rusty E. Frank, *Tap!* Da Capo Press, c. 1994, pg. 195

65   Rusty E. Frank, *Tap!* Da Capo Press, c. 1994, pg. 198

66   Sheldon Winkler, *The Music of World War II*, Merriam Pr. NY, c. 2013, pg. 13

67   Rusty E. Frank, *Tap!* Da Capo Press, c. 1994, pg. 201

68   Alan Anderson, *The Songwriter Goes to War*, Limelight Ed., c. 2004, pg. 188

69   Andrew Glass, "Truman Ends Racial Segregation in Armed Forces," Politico, July 26, 2018 (This article mentions the

resistance of some military brass to the enforcement of desegregation. The last all-black military unit wasn't abolished until September, 1954)

70 Jay Price, "A Shocking Discovery About Lynchings: Military Veterans Often Were Targets," BBC World News, September 24, 2018; Equal Justice Initiative, *Lynching in America: Targeting Black Americans*, c. 2017

71 Robert Sidney, *With Malice Towards Some*, 1st Book Library, c. 2003, pg. 13

72 Rusty E. Frank, *Tap!* Da Capo Press, c. 1994, pgs. 195-198 (Gene penned the bulk of Chapter 20, submitting it to author Frank on June 6, 1989)

73 Richard Goldstein, *Helluva Town: The Story of New York City During World War II*, Simon and Schuster, c. 2010, pg. 160

**Chapter Four**

74 Miriam Nelson, "I Married a Serviceman," *Photoplay*, February 1952

75 Miriam Nelson, *My Life Dancing with the Stars*, BearManor, c. 2009, pg. 76

76 Rusty E. Frank, *Tap!* De Capo Press, c. 1994, pg. 198

77 Fredda Dudley, "How a Star is Born," *Photoplay*, December 1950

78 *Variety*, March 6, 1946 – mention of Gene Berg's name change

79 Rusty E. Frank, *Tap!* De Capo Press, c. 1994, pgs. 198-199

80 Rusty E. Frank, *Tap!* De Capo Press, c. 1994, pg. 199

81 Ida Zeitlin, "Cheerful Little Earful," *Modern Screen*, October 1946

82 June Haver, "3 Queens for a Day," *Screenland*, March 1947

83 Tony Thomas, *That's Dancing!* Abrams Press, c. 1984, pg. 219

84 David Soren, "Joseph E. Howard: Vaudeville, Broadway and Television", University of Arizona, Arizona.edu

85   Leonard Maltin, *Classic Movie Guide*, Plume (3rd ed.), c. 2015, pg. 342

86   Jacqueline T. Lynch, review of *I Wonder Who's Kissing Her Now*, anotheroldmovieblog, April 6, 2017

87   "Top Grossers of 1947," *Variety*, January 7, 1948

88   T.N.T., review of *I Wonder Who's Kissing Her Now? The Post Standard* (Syracuse, N.Y.) July 24, 1947

89   John Franceschina, *Hermes Pan: The Man Who Danced with Fred Astaire*, Oxford Univ. Pr. c. 2012, pg. 148 (Pan's statement was mentioned in a 1947 issue of the San Francisco publication *Opera, Concert and Symphony*)

90   Rusty E. Frank, *Tap!* De Capo Press, c. 1994, pg. 199

91   Miriam Nelson, *My Life Dancing with the Stars*, BearManor, c. 2009, pg. 78

92   California Birth Index, 1950-1993, Vol. 2

93   David Parkinson, *The Rough Guide to Film Musicals*, Penguin, c. 2007, pg. 90

94   Fredda Dudley, "How a Star is Born," *Photoplay*, December 1950

95   William J. Mann, *Behind the Screen*, Viking Press, c. 2001, pg. 261

96   "At Liberty," *Motion Picture Herald*, July 10, 1948

97   John Anthony Gilvey, *Before the Parade Passes By: Gower Champion and the Glorious American Musical*, St. Martin's, c. 2005, pg. 35

98   Carol Channing, *Just Lucky I Guess – A Memoir of Sorts*, Simon & Schuster, c. 2002, pg. 58

99   Miriam Nelson, *My Life Dancing with the Stars*, BearManor, c. 2009, pg. 80

100  Dorothy Kilgallen, "Voice of Broadway," news column, November 1, 1948

101 Miriam Nelson, *My Life Dancing with the Stars*, BearManor, c. 2009, pg. 80

102 Mark Barron, "*Lend an Ear* Wins Broadway Praise," Associated Pr. review, December 21, 1948

103 Bill Riley, *Lend an Ear* review, *Billboard*, December 2, 1948 (from Boston tryout)

104 Rusty E. Frank, *Tap!* De Capo Press, c. 1994, pg. 199


**Chapter Five**

105 Miriam Nelson (as Mrs. Gene Nelson), "How I Pursued My Husband," *Photoplay* (July 1951)

106 Mary Nash, review of *The Daughter of Rosie O'Grady*, *Buffalo Evening News*, April 20, 1950

107 John A. Gallagher, Director/Actor Gene Nelson Talks Hollywood, (Interview – tvdays.com – Youtube) c.1982

108 "Gene Nelson Booked for the Music Hall," *Brooklyn Eagle*, February 4, 1950

109 "Speaking of Pictures," *Life* magazine, August 15, 1949 (Photos were taken in New York, prior to Gene, Miriam and Chris returning to Hollywood)

110 David Kaufman, *Doris Day – The Untold Story of the Girl Next Door*, Virgin Bks., c. 2008, pg. 98 (original quote from a June 1950 interview with James Padgitt of the *Dallas Times Herald*)

111 Liza Wilson, Program Notes for review of *Tea for Two*, *Photoplay*, October 1950

112 Miriam Nelson, *My Life Dancing With the Stars*, BearManor, c. 2009, pg. 84

113 Miriam Nelson, *My Life Dancing With the Stars*, BearManor, c. 2009, pg. 80

114 "Dancing Feet Go Miles in One Day," *Times-Union* (NY), December 3, 1950

115  Archer Winsten, review of *Tea for Two*, *New York Post*, September 3, 1950

116  BARN, review of *Tea for Two*, *Film Bulletin*, August 28, 1950

117  Jeanine Basinger, *The Movie Musical!* Knopf, c. 2019, pg. 201

118  Gene Nelson interview, Skip E. Lowe Looks at Hollywood, (weekly TV talk show, 1990)

119  Leonard Maltin, *Classic Movie Guide, 3rd Edition*, Plume, c. 2015, pg. 771

120  A.E. Hotchner, *Doris Day – Her Own Story*, Bantam, c. 1975, pg. 176

121  Garry McGee, *Doris Day – Sentimental Journey*, McFarland, c. 2015, pg. 21

122  James Robert Parish, Michael R. Pitts, *Hollywood Songsters: Garland to O'Connor, Vol. 2*, Taylor & Francis, c. 2003, pg. 370

123  Roby Heard, "The June Haver Story," *Long-Island Star Journal*, February 16, 1953

124  Walt., review of *Lullaby of Broadway*, *Variety*, March 14, 1951

125  Howard Pollack, *George Gershwin: His Life and Work*, University of California Pr., c. 2006, pg. 757

126  Tony Thomas, *That's Dancing!* Abrams Press, c. 1984, pg. 222

127  A.E. Hotchner, *Doris Day – Her Own Story*, Bantam, c. 1975, pgs. 146-147

128  Sidney Skolsky, Hollywood is My Beat, *New York Post*, June 24, 1951

129  Miriam Nelson, *My Life Dancing With the Stars*, BearManor, c. 2009, pg. 90

130  Paul O'Neill, "The 'Clan' is the Most," *Life* magazine, December 22, 1958 (Details Bogart's "Holmby Hills Rat Pack") (On August 5, 1950, columnist Erskine Johnson quoted Bogart saying, "We're the middle-aged hot rod club of the Beverly Hills Rat Pack")

131 Jan Hoffman, "Public Lives; A Dancer's 8-Decade Arc to Top Banana," *The New York Times*, July 14, 1999

**Chapter Six**

132 David Butler, Irene Kahn Atkins, *David Butler*, Scarecrow Pr., c. 1993, pg. 243 (interview conducted in 1977)

133 Robert J. Lentz, *Korean War Filmography*, McFarland, c. 2003

134 John Howard Reid, *More Movie Musicals*, lulu.com, c. 2006, pg. 194

135 Gene Nelson, "Our Christmas Love Story," *Modern Screen*, January 1952

136 "No Help at All," *Buffalo Evening News*, December 22, 1951

137 "Hollywood," *Variety*, January 9, 1952

138 California Deaths and Burials, 1776-2000

139 Zabe, "New Acts – Gene Nelson," *Variety*, February 27, 1952

140 "Warner – New York," *Variety*, April 9, 1952

141 "Newsmen Honor Leigh," *Motion Picture Daily*, April 18, 1952

142 Lawrence J. Mullen, *Las Vegas: Media and Myth*, Lexington Bks., c. 2007, pg. 11

143 Miriam Nelson, *My Life Dancing with the Stars*, BearManor, c. 2009, pgs. 90-91

144 Bosley Crowther, review of *She's Working Her Way Through College*, *New York Times*, July 10, 1952

145 Virginia Mayo, *The Best Years of My Life*, Beachhouse Books, c. 2001, Chapter 22

146 Tony Thomas, *That's Dancing!* Abrams Press, c. 1984, pg. 223

147 Review, "She's Working Her Way Through College," *Seattle Daily Times*, July 16, 1952

148 Max Baer Show, radio interview with Gene Nelson, circa 1952

149 James Robert Parish, *Forties Gals*, Arlington House, c. 1980, pg. 222

150  Tony Thomas, *That's Dancing!* Abrams Press, c. 1984, pg. 223

151  William R. Weaver, review of *She's Back on Broadway*, *Motion Picture Daily*, January 23, 1953

152  "Father of Dancer Succumbs at 67," *Salt Lake Tribune*, August 9, 1952

153  "WB Launches Heaviest Hue Program," *Film Bulletin*, November 3, 1952

154  *Film Noir Reader 3: Interviews with Filmmakers of the Classic Noir Period*, Hal Leonard Corp., c. 2002, pg. 21

155  Laura Wagner, review of *Crime Wave*, Laura's Miscellaneous Musings (on-line), April 13, 2013

156  Mildred Martin, review of *Crime Wave*, *Philadelphia Inquirer*, April 3, 1954

157  Cal York (pseudonym for *Photoplay* editorials), "Inside Stuff," *Photoplay* October 1953

158  Janet Graves, review of *The City is Dark*, *Photoplay*, September 1953


**Chapter Seven**

159  *Three Sailors and a Girl*, review, *Harrison Reports*, November 28, 1953

160  H.H.T., review of *Three Sailors and a Girl*, *New York Times*, November 23, 1953

161  John A. Gallagher, Director/Actor Gene Nelson Talks Hollywood, (Interview – tvdays.com -Youtube) c. 1982

162  Jane Powell, *The Girl Next Door ... and How She Grew*, William Morrow and Co., c. 1988

163  Jane Powell, *The Girl Next Door ... and How She Grew*, William Morrow and Co., c. 1988

164  Jane Powell, *The Girl Next Door ... and How She Grew*, William Morrow and Co., c. 1988

165 "Jane Powell Wins Divorce," *Times-Union*, August 7, 1953 (Powell's divorce became final on August 6, 1954)

166 Miriam Nelson, *My Life Dancing with the Stars*, BearManor, c. 2009, pg. 95

167 "Piazza Vs. Christine," *Variety*, May 13, 1953 (The term "transexual" was used at the time)

168 Miriam Nelson, *My Life Dancing with the Stars*, BearManor, c. 2009, pg. 96

169 Miriam Nelson, *My Life Dancing with the Stars*, BearManor, c. 2009, pg. 97

170 Michael Buckley, "Jane Powell," *Films in Review*, June-July 1987

171 Jane Powell, *The Girl Next Door ... and How She Grew*, William Morrow and Co., c. 1988

172 Michael Buckley, "Jane Powell," *Films in Review*, June-July 1987

173 Dorothy Kilgallen, "Exclusive Movie Gossip," *Screenland*, November 1953

174 "Stars in Action," *Photoplay*, July 1954

175 Tony Thomas, *The Films of Gene Kelly*, Citadel Press, c. 1991, pg. 20

176 Tony Curtis, Peter Golenbock, *American Prince: A Memoir*, Crown, c. 2008, pg. 165

177 York, *So This is Paris* review, *Film Bulletin*, December 13, 1954

178 Archer Winsten, *So This is Paris* review, *New York Post*, February 13, 1955

179 Howard McClay, "Nelson Tells Fairbanks Influence," *Daily News*, May 7, 1954

180 Tony Thomas, *That's Dancing!* Harry N. Abrams Inc., c. 1984, pg. 225

181 "Briefs from the Lots," *Variety*, December 8, 1954

182 Tony Curtis, Peter Golenbock, *American Prince: A Memoir*, Crown, c. 2008, pg. 165

**Chapter Eight**

183 Sheilah Graham, "Hollywood Diary", *Buffalo Evening News*, August 23, 1954

184 Tony Thomas, *That's Dancing!* Harry N. Abrams, Inc., c. 1984, pg. 225

185 John A. Gallagher, Director/Actor Gene Nelson Talks Hollywood, (Interview – tvdays.com – Youtube) c. 1982

186 Gene Triplett, "Oklahoma! sweeps plains in BIG, bright living color," *The Oklahoman*, June 30, 1983

187 Tony Thomas, *That's Dancing!* Harry N. Abrams, Inc., c. 1984, pg. 225

188 Robert J. Lentz, *Gloria Grahame – Bad Girl of Film Noir*, McFarland, c. 2011, pg. 192

189 Robert J. Lentz, *Gloria Grahame – Bad Girl of Film Noir*, McFarland, c. 2011, pg. 192

190 William K. Zinsser, review of *Oklahoma!*, *Buffalo Evening News*, October 11, 1955

191 William R. Weaver, review of *Oklahoma!*, *Motion Picture Herald*, October 8, 1955

192 Review of *Oklahoma!*, *Variety*, March 26, 1958

193 Earl Wilson, "Anyway, New York City Still Has Great Parties," *Galveston Daily News*, March 30, 1972

194 Gene Triplett, "Oklahoma! sweeps plains in BIG, bright living color," *The Oklahoman*, June 30, 1983

195 Charles Epstein, Critics Corner, *Jewish Post*, July 13, 1983

196 "Shocker!" *The Daily Herald*, January 27, 1955

197 Janne Wass, review of *The Atomic Man*, scifist.wordpress.com, January 13, 2017

198 Details provided from "List of In-Bound Passengers" for the Queen Mary (it was noted on the manifest that Gene and Lenore "did not embark")

199 Review of "Broadway," *Variety*, May 11, 1955

200 Steven Scheurer, "Gene Nelson Prefers TV Spot to Broadway," *Long Island Star-Journal*, May 13, 1955

201 Piper Laurie, *Learning to Live Out Loud: A Memoir*, Crown, c. 2011, pgs. 138-139

202 Review of *Dial 999*, *Today's Cinema*, December 9, 1955

203 Review of *The Way Out*, *Film Bulletin*, April 30, 1956

204 Sheliah Graham column, November 23, 1955

205 Piper Laurie, *Learning to Live Out Loud: A Memoir*, Crown, c. 2011, pgs. 140-141

**Chapter Nine**

206 Review of "Tryout," *Variety*, October 5, 1955

207 Tony Thomas, *That's Dancing!*, Abrams Press, c. 1984, pg. 226

208 Piper Laurie, *Learning to Live Out Loud: A Memoir*, Crown, c. 2011, pg. 143 (Hollywood correspondent Helen Louise Walker mentioned Schine's reluctance to be photographed with Piper – in a May 1956 issue of *Screenland*)

209 "Loved Widely and Too Well, Now He's Solo," *The New York Post*, June 8, 1956

210 Miriam Nelson, *My Life Dancing with the Stars*, BearManor, c. 2009, pg. 136

211 *Foolin' Ourselves*, review, *Variety*, January 23, 1957

212 *Darling, I'm Yours*, review, *Variety*, May 15, 1957

213 Tony Thomas, *That's Dancing!*, Abrams Press, c. 1984, pgs. 225-226

214 "Gene Nelson's Injuries On Location Prompts 75G Suit Versus Panorama," *Variety*, November 5, 1957

215 Tony Thomas, *That's Dancing!*, Abrams Press, c. 1984, pg. 226

216  TV Key Previews, *Albany-Times* (NY), May 1, 1958

217  Val Holley, *Mike Connolly and the Manly Art of Hollywood Gossip*, McFarland, c. 2010, pgs. 17, 22

218  Mike Connolly, "Mr. Hollywood" column, *Star-News*, August 14, 1958

219  Frances Ingram, "Gene Nelson – Athletic Grace," *Classic Images*, December 2005

220  "Continue 'Hit the Deck' A Week at Jones Beach," *Variety*, September 7, 1960

221  Walter Hawver, "Shangri-La': Very Best," *Knickerbocker News*, October 23, 1960


**Chapter Ten**

222  W.E. J. M., review of *20,000 Eyes*, *Buffalo Co0urier-Experess*, July 15, 1961

223  Review of *20,000 Eyes*, *Variety*, July 5, 1961

224  Review of *The Purple Hills*, *Variety*, October 25, 1961

225  Tom Weaver, *I Talked with a Zombie: Interviews with Horror and Sci-Fi Films*, McFarland, c. 2009, pg. 109

226  "Gene Nelson Wins $72,675; 1957 Horse Fall Damages," *Variety*, June 28, 1961

227  Tom Weaver, *Interviews with B Science Fiction and Horror Movie Makers*, McFarland, c. 1988, pg. 11

228  Tom Weaver, *I Talked with a Zombie: Interviews with Horror and Sci-Fi Films*, McFarland, c. 2009, pgs. 115-116

229  "It's Official! He's Gene Nelson," (AP) *Albany Times-Union*, June 17, 1964

230  Marc Eliot, *Nicholson: A Biography*, Crown, c. 2014, pgs. 40-41

231  Review of *Thunder Island*, *Variety*, October 2, 1963

232  Marc Eliot, *Nicholson: A Biography*, Crown, c. 2014, pg. 41

233 Review of "Who Killed Vaudeville?" *Bingingham Press*, September 23, 1964

234 Conversation with Gary Conway, December 12, 2022

235 In 1959 Nelson appeared in two MGM series: *Northwest Passage*, and *Bat Masterson*

236 Philip K. Scheuer, "Nelson Up a Rung on Director Ladder," *Los Angeles Times*, September 10, 1963

237 Gene Nelson interview, Skip E. Lowe Looks at Hollywood, (weekly TV talk show, 1990)

238 Review of *Hootenanny Hoot, Variety*, August 28, 1963

239 Robert Burke Warren, *Cash on Cash: Interviews and Encounters with Johnny Cash*, Chicago Review Pr., c. 2022, pg. 159 (from 1987 interview with Robert K. Oermann)

240 Jason Schneider, *Whispering Pines: The Northern Roots of American Music*, ECW Pr., c. 2010

241 Gene Nelson interview, Skip E. Lowe Looks at Hollywood, (weekly TV talk show, 1990)

242 Jerry Hopkins, *Elvis: The Biography*, Plexus Pub., c. 2014 (Nelson interview with Hopkins)

243 Peter Guralnick, *Careless Love: The Unmaking of Elvis Presley*, Little, Brown & Co., c. 1999

244 Gene Nelson interview, Skip E. Lowe Looks at Hollywood, (weekly TV talk show, 1990)

245 Jerry Hopkins, *Elvis: The Biography*, Plexus Pub., c. 2014

246 James L. Neibaur, *The Elvis Movies*, Rowen & Littlefield, c. 2014, pg. 139

247 James L. Neibaur, *The Elvis Movies*, Rowen & Littlefield, c. 2014, pg. 81

248 David Fantle, *Hollywood Heyday: 75 Candid Interviews with Golden Age Legends*, McFarland, c. 2018

249 Leonard Maltin, *Leonard Maltin's Movie & Video Guide*, Penguin, c. 1997, pg. 1531 (rated *** stars)

250  George Hamilton, *Don't Mind if I Do*, Simon & Schuster, c. 2008, pg. 182

251  Review of *Your Cheatin' Heart*, *Motion Picture Exhibitor*, October 21, 1964

252  Howard Thompson, review of *Your Cheatin' Heart*, *New York Times*, May 20, 1965

253  John Douglas Eames, *The MGM Story*, Crown Pub., c. 1975, pg. 327

254  Peter Guralnick, *Careless Love: The Unmaking of Elvis Presley*, Little, Brown & Co., c. 1999

255  Peter Guralnick, *Careless Love: The Unmaking of Elvis Presley*, Little, Brown & Co., c. 1999

**Chapter 11**

256  Sidney Sheldon, *The Other Side of Me*, Grand Central Pub., c. 2006, Chapter 31

257  Steve Cox and Howard Frank, *Dreaming of Jeannie: TV's Prime Time in a Bottle*, St. Martin's, c. 2000

258  Barbara Eden, *Jeannie Out of the Bottle: A Memoir*, Crown, c. 2011

259  Larry Hagman, Todd Gold, *Hello Darlin': Tall (and Absolutely True) Tales About My Life*, Simon & Schuster, c. 2001, pgs. 127-130

260  Barbara Eden, *Jeannie Out of the Bottle: A Memoir*, Crown, c. 2011, pg. 148

261  Barbara Eden, *Jeannie Out of the Bottle: A Memoir*, Crown, c. 2011, pg. 148

262  Television Academy Interviews, An Oral History of Television, Sidney Sheldon, March 30, 2000

263  Stephen Cox, *Dreaming of Jeannie*, St. Martin's Pr., c. 2000

264  Doug Brown, "'The Cool Ones' Getting Warmed Up," *Desert Sun*, July 26, 1966

265  Charles Tranberg, *William Conrad: A Life & Career*, BearManor Media, c. 2018

266  Bosley Crowther, review of *The Cool Ones*, *New York Times*, May 11, 1967

267  Peggy Lipton, *Breathing Out: A Memoir*, St. Martins, c. 2007, pg. 137

268  Marc Cushman, Susan Osborn, *These Are the Voyages-TOS: Season Two*, Jacob Brown Media, c. 2014, pg. 448

269  Leonard Nimoy, Sci-Fi Channel, Star Trek Special Edition, Star-Trek Insights, "Gamesters of Triskelion," 1998-99

270  Gene's interview, *The Merv Griffin Show*, Hollywood Palace Theater, July 31, 1972

271  Marian Christy, "Gene Nelson: Back in Full Swing," *The Journal News*, July 8, 1971

272  Bob Avian, *Dancing Man: A Broadway Choreographer's Journey*, Univ. Pr. of Mississippi, c. 2020

273  Harold Prince, *Sense of Occasion-Harold Prince*, Applause Theatre & Cinema Books, c. 2017

274  Ted Chapin, *Everything was Possible: The Birth of the Musical Follies*, Rowman and Littlefield, c. 2005

275  Matt Weinstock, *Arts*, *Paris Review*, November 29, 2013

276  Poll conducted by the producers of ABC's "Hollywood: The Dream Factory" (January 1972) (a.k.a. The American Entertainment Awards)

277  Michael Misita, Broadway Remembered (Facebook), March 25, 2023 (Misita told me that it was "wonderful" that I was writing a biography for Gene Nelson)

278  Matt Weinstock, "Arts," *The Paris Review*, November 29, 2013

279  John Kenneth Muir, *Terror Television*, McFarland, c. 2013

280  Dominic McHugh, *Alan Jay Lerner: A Lyricist's Letters*, Oxford Univ. Pr., c. 2014 (some sources say that Dailey had a tendon injury)

281 William Glover, review of *Music! Music!*, *Observer-Dispatch*, April 13, 1974

282 Frances Ingram, "Gene Nelson – Athletic Grace," *Classic Images*, December 2005

283 Miriam Nelson, *My Life Dancing with the Stars*, BearManor, c. 2009, pg. 298

284 Jane Lenz Elder, *Alice Faye-A Life Beyond the Silver Screen*, Univ. Press of Mississippi., c. 2002, pg. 221

285 Donald McLean, review of *Good News*, *Bay Area Reporter*, May 15, 1974

286 Clive Barnes, review for *Good News*, *New York Times*, December 24, 1974


**Chapter 12**

287 Robin Adams Sloan (Roberta Ashley), "Maureen Reagan dates a 56-year-old", *Sun Telegram* (San Bernardino), August 4, 1976

288 Kitty Kelley, *Nancy Reagan-The Unauthorized Biography*, Simon & Schuster, c. 1991, pg. 224 (from Kelley's October 1988 interviews with Gene Nelson)

289 Anne Edwards, *The Reagans: Portrait of a Marriage*, Roman & Littlefield, c. 2018, pg. 114

290 Seth Rosenfield, *Subversives: The FBI's War on Student Radicals, and Reagan's Rise to Power, Farrar, Straus, & Giroux, c. 2012. pg. 511*

291 Kitty Kelley, *Nancy Reagan-The Unauthorized Biography*, Simon & Schuster, c. 1991, pg. 224 (from Kelley's October 1988 interviews with Gene Nelson)

292 Kitty Kelley, *Nancy Reagan-The Unauthorized Biography*, Simon & Schuster, c. 1991, pg. 224 (from Kelley's October 1988 interviews with Gene Nelson)

293 Kitty Kelley, *Nancy Reagan-The Unauthorized Biography*, Simon & Schuster, c. 1991, pg. 224 (from Kelley's October 1988 interviews with Gene Nelson)

294 Michael Reagan, *On the Outside Looking In*, Kensington Pub. Corp., c. 1989, pg. 202

295 Frances Ingram, "Gene Nelson – Athletic Grace," *Classic Images*, December 2005

296 Jan Wahl, conversation with author (January 31, 2023)

297 Jan Wahl, email to author (April 17, 2023)

298 Gene Nelson interview, Skip E. Lowe Looks at Hollywood, (weekly TV talk show, 1990)

299 Gene Nelson interview, Skip E. Lowe Looks at Hollywood, (weekly TV talk show, 1990)

300 Rob Lopez, "Oscar night … Or a trip to Oz," *Sausalito Marin Scope*, April 11, 1989

301 Jan Wahl, conversation with author (January 31, 2023)

302 Brian, "Exclusive Interview with Rusty Frank," Swingdance. LA, September 21, 2017

303 Kevin Wedman, Warner Bros. – First National Pictures, Facebook

304 Social column, *San Mateo Times*, June 20, 1974

305 C. Michael Traw, Broadway Remembered (Facebook), March 25, 2023

306 Miriam Nelson, *My Life Dancing with the Stars*, BearManor, c. 2009, pg. 305

307 Victoria Gordo, Facebook post, dated October 8, 2015

308 Gene Nelson interview, Skip E. Lowe Looks at Hollywood, (weekly TV talk show, 1990) (Gene gave no specifics as to the choices he would have reconsidered).

309 Marian Christy, "Gene Nelson: Back in Full Swing," *The Journal News*, July 8, 1971

310 Rusty E. Frank, *Tap!* Da Capo Pr., c. 1990, pg. 201

## Afterword

311 "Miriam Nelson, Dancer and Choreographer for 7 Decades, Dies at 98," *The Hollywood Reporter*, August 20, 2018

312 James Robert Parish, e-mail dated August 19, 2022

# Index